This book is dedicated to those who came before us: Rose Basile Green, Jerre Mangione, Olga Peragallo, Remigio Pane, Peter Sammartino, Giovanni Schiavo, Felix Stefanile, Rudolph Vecoli, and others who made sure that the field continued to thrive....

TABLE OF CONTENTS

PREFACE

This collection is the result of a three and one-half day conference that took place in March 2014 at the Rockefeller Foundation Center in Bellagio, Italy. Funded entirely by the Foundation, eighteen scholars met from 9:30 AM to 6:00 PM for three days in order to analyze the current status of the field of Italian-American studies in both Italy and the United States and to examine further the possibilities of what the future might hold.

The immediate results of the meeting were twofold: first, the creation of the Italian-American Studies Network; second, the idea to create an initial working document, which is the book you now hold in your hands. We do not presume to offer herein all of the answers to the challengers facing Italian Americana in both countries. Our initial intentions at this juncture are to shed light on what the current situation is and, in some cases, how we might contribute to the further success in the promotion of the field.

Two are the immediate challenges, in our opinion; and it is, to some degree, a question of what comes first, the chicken or the egg. One, we need to be sure that new scholars enrolled in doctoral programs have the opportunity to be trained in Italian Americana, that they are able to enroll in courses in their respective programs. This, to be sure, is more of a philosophical-ideological issue. Two, there is a dire need for courses to be offered at the graduate (preferably, doctorate) level so that students indeed have the opportunity to take courses and, when possible, declare a concentration in Italian Americana within their degree program, be it American Studies, Anthropology, History, Italian, Political Science, Psychology, Sociology, etc. This is the only way to insure that an academic legacy of the history and culture is passed along to future generations.

Indeed, as Gardaphé tells us in his essay herein, that while there is still no formal program leading to a doctorate in Italian-American studies, he and I have developed graduate courses in the field at Queens College through the Master of Liberal Arts and Italian Master's Degree programs. Further still, for more than twenty-five years, together with the likes of Professors Mary Jo Bona, Philip Cannistraro, Donna Gabaccia, Rudolph Vecoli, Pasquale Verdicchio, Virgina Yans, and Robert Viscusi, we have directed and served on dissertation committees for students both in the U.S. and in Italy. We have also taught graduate and undergraduate courses at Purdue University, Columbia College Chicago, CUNY Graduate Center, Florida Atlantic University, Stony Brook University, University of Minnesota, and Brooklyn College, among others, enabling a new generation of scholars to develop in subsequent years. In the past two years, Gardaphé and I have taught Italian-American studies at the University of Perugia for Foreigners and the University of Calabria, where, in this second university, together with Professors Margherita Ganeri and Marta Petrusewicz, we have created a seminar in Italian-American studies that is required for all graduate students in modern and contemporary Italian literature.

These are some models other programs can both emulate and/or use as a blue print for their own programs. As we write, no doctoral program in the United States, for instance, allows students to add Italian-American studies as part of their course of study. This is true for both English departments and Italian departments. Such an observation, of course, raises the other issue as to where Italian-American studies should reside. At Purdue University, in West Lafayette, Indiana, doctoral students in both American studies and Comparative Literature could opt for Italian Americana as part of their course of studies. Similarly, at Florida Atlantic University, students in the Ph.D. Program for Comparative Studies had the option of Italian Americana as part of their course of studies. In fact, all three of the above-mentioned programs have had students go on to a career in the university and, with the usual revisions one often brings to their dissertations, went on to publish books with a variety of university presses (e.g., Fairleigh Dickinson University Press, Fordham University Press, SUNY

Press). Students from Stony Book University, as well, have gone on to publish their revised dissertations as books with other academic presses.

As one might readily notice, the bulk of these institutions are not from the Northeast, an area with a large Italian-American population. Except for one dissertation in the English department and three in the History department of the CUNY Graduate Center, within the New York Tri-State Metropolitan Area, Italian-American studies remains absent from any Ph.D. program as an option for doctoral students.

With the belief that such a program of formal study matters, and in the interest of eliciting support from both the academic and social communities, we offer this volume in the hopes that it will stimulate further thought that will, in the end, manifest itself in action that will insure the institutionalization of Italian-American history and culture at the university level.

Finally, we wish to thank the Rockefeller Foundation for their support in making this project possible and the following individuals for assisting with a seamlessly smooth process of bringing it to fruition: Peter J. Madonia, Rob Garris, and Laura Podio of the Rockefeller Foundation both here and in Bellagio, and David D'Amato, Director of Development at Queens College.

Fred L. Gardaphé
Anthony Julian Tamburri
New York, Winter 2015

ITALIAN AMERICAN LITERARY STUDIES AT BELLAGIO

Robert Viscusi
BROOKLYN COLLEGE, CUNY

for Mary Jo Bona

Four years ago, returning to New York from Milano, I changed flights at Heathrow. To get from one plane to another that would depart from the same building, I had to go through security three separate times. On the last of these three, the inspector opened my carry-on bag. "What's this, then?" he said, "Books?" He took them out, one after another, ten copies of a bilingual edition of a poem called *Ellis Island.* He laid them out on the table, like evidence of a crime, and stared at me. "I'm a writer," I said. "These are copies of my book."

He stared a little longer and then let me pass through. I went away with the uneasy feeling that I had been excused an infraction. We had no actual discussion. I don't know whether he noticed what my book was about. But I recognized his suspicion. Many, perhaps most, writers would recognize it. And not least, those of us who write about immigrants and their posterity. Italian American writing, like all immigrant writing, I thought, cannot help breaking rules.

This essay accepts three facts that appear mutually contradictory. *First fact*. Italian American Literary Studies were first kept in colonial silos, like the Sicilians in the New Orleans jail, "for their own safety." But they were always trying to escape. Later they were kept in national silos. American Studies, likewise, have lived under the protection of geopolitical agendas. *Second fact*. These silos, all appearances to the contrary notwithstanding, have always been interdependent. But the silos are important. *Third fact.* The colonial silos that underlie them never go away, and they constitute a persistent obstacle to the kinds of exchange we are talking about at this conference.

"NATIONAL" SILOS

Nations belong to a system of world exchange, readily visualized by an arc of flags outside an Olympic Stadium or the Secretariat of the United

From: *Transcending Borders, Bridging Gaps* (Calandra Institute, 2015)

Nations. But nations are paradoxical actors. To be sure, they engage on the paved grounds and open fields of world commerce, gauging their progress and their rankings by indices of international exchange, which cover many arenas of production from manufacturing to finance to popular music to high culture to hockey teams. But the comparatist and competitive features of the international system encourage all participants to practice secrecy and tactical exclusion of both enemies and friends.

Furthermore, the production of national silos, whether in the direction of sports teams or the development of research collaboratives, shows the effects of physical inertia. It is a thousand ways easier to recruit high-school sports teams in one's own borough than it would be to seek for candidates on the other side of the world: barriers of distance, language, and finance have many avenues of intervention. What is true of high-school centers and forwards is equally true of research assistants in emerging disciplines. A proper *équipe* in Italian American studies would include researchers from Italy and all the Americas, indeed all of the national communities that speak what used to be exclusively European languages.

No one has yet assembled such a team of graduate students and assistant professors. But that day may not be as far off as one might imagine.

The Interdependence of Silos

Scholarship in the humanities is irreducibly international. Despite centuries of patriotism, exceptionalism, and other forms of geopolitical isolation, students of literature have voracious appetites for languages other than the ones they learned from their mothers, and for stories that come from places they have never visited, for letters from people they can never meet. Humanist scholarship in immigrant and post-immigrant literatures is doubly international, both because it belongs to humanism and because it is based in international movements of peoples. There is no purity in such literatures. They grow out of linguistic contamination no less than out of dislocation and strife.

At this meeting, there is the clear possibility of a new level of conscious interdependence. Everyone here is aware of the contributions of such initiatives as *Altreitalie,* the publications of Emilio Franzina, Graziella Parati, Gian Antonio Stella. Nonetheless this history is littered with difficulties, and it is to these that I now turn.

Obstacles to Interdependence

Colonial Silos.

The early history of Italian American literary studies is a history of colonial production, which operates, a silo within a silo, under a heavy cloak of protection. Four examples of how this has worked in practice:

1. *Closed circuits of communication.*

In a strictly colonial situation, like that of Italian American writing during the period of mass migration (1880-1923), literary studies were focused on metropolitan concerns. The Italian language, Italian political history, Italian authority, and, in general, working relationships with Italian cultural and administrative institutions were basic to the survival of colonial newspapers and publishers. Often, even the Italian American left was more passionately concerned with Italian politics than with the politics of the colony or with those of the colony's host country.

2. *Antiquated models of ideology.*

Reading the colonial newspapers, one finds continual signs of a closed and immobile culture. The colonials were encouraged to perpetuate the Italian language and Italian culture. This generally meant, in literature, the study of Dante Alighieri—the nineteenth century's protonationalist par excellence. In the later colonial period, Fascist propaganda found a wide and ready audience in the colonia, where it appealed, as it had done in Italy, to the resentments and injuries that Italians felt on any political stage, whether at the treaty conference of Versailles or in USAmerican public and corporate discourse.

3. *Repression of new ideas.*

Readers were discouraged from entertaining new ideas that pertained to the conduct of daily life. One sees this in the liberation of women. During the colonial period of Italian life in the United States, this was a bitter struggle. Even the Futurist Marinetti inveighed against the introduction of pastasciutta because it lessened women's work and weakened the mystique of the Italian home, which rested upon fresh pasta. The newspapers often hosted debates about freedom to choose the means of production of family life, in every matter from styles of clothing and of courtship to the machinery used or not used in housekeeping.

4. *Underfunding.*

Colonial institutions of literature were almost entirely dependent upon newspaper circulation. In the 1920s, every now and then, a determined immigrant writer, like Emanuel Carnevali or Pascal D'Angelo, managed to gain access to American means of communication, but these remained exceptional. In the thirties, these exceptions were more numerous—John Fante, Jerre Mangione, Pietro Di Donato, Mari Tomasi managed to break out of the closed circuits of the colonial world. But there was little systematic access to wider networks.

Postcolonial Silos.

1. *Interruptions.*

Strictly speaking, the colonial period ended with Mussolini's declaration of war against the United States in December 1941. Italian colonial policy had worked to keep the Italian language alive among immigrant communities. Now the federal government of the USA put up posters in those same communities commanding "Don't speak the Enemy's Language! Speak American!" And the Italian Americans complied.

Italians in Boston, New York, Philadelphia, Denver, San Francisco, Chicago, New Haven, Saint Louis stopped trying to convince their Americanizing children to maintain the Italian language. This meant that an important part of the colonial circuit was interrupted, for the most part fatally. It also meant that postcolonial Italian America would have very little to do with postwar Italy. This development too proceeded with a certain fatality.

2. *Antiquated Models of Ideology.*

It was clear after the war that Italian political and cultural policy were not going to play much of a role in the production of Italian American literary studies. Italian Americans once more displayed a deep attraction for antiquated models of ideology, though not the same ones as those that had appealed to them before the war. Now Americanism, whether in its trades-union overalls or in its Republican fear of foreigners and left-wing ideas, captured many Italian Americans and their spiritual advisors.

3. *Repression of New Ideas.*

The cosmopolitan world of university intellectuals and major-league publishers did not include many visible Italian Americans, and those who found their way into those precincts often felt deeply uncomfortable there. They hid behind assumed names (Francesca Vinciguerra as Frances Winwar or Salvatore Lombino as Ed McBain) or they exhibited a very visible touchiness about being call Italian Americans (the most famous example is John Ciardi's objection to Robert Lowell's praising him for being the best Italian American poet). Even these writers were rare adventurers. Many more Italian American reputations did not survive the postwar period unharmed. Di Donato spent much of the war detained for his status as conscientious objector, and afterwards had great difficulty finding publishers. Vito Marcantonio, long a successful representative from Italian Harlem, was brutally defeated when he ran for Mayor of New York City in 1949.

4. *Underfunding.*

Always a difficult subject, Italian American philanthropy turned away from political and cultural ideas that might have been considered suspect under the paranoid klieg lights of congressional hearings in the 1950s. Movie stars avoided their friends. Universities let people go. Italian Americans with money turned to medical research and Catholic Charities, not to troublesome writers and intellectuals.

Global Italian America

It is possible to imagine that we have been speaking only of the bad old days. Many things have improved. That we are here together in this splendid place and for this forward-thinking purpose is perhaps the best sign that the new age, with its improved communications, its abandonment of many borders, and its expertise in cross-cultural collaboration has made possible new levels of understanding and of progress. *Nonostante tutto, comunque, ci resta molto da fare.*

1. *Open Circuits.*

Where there were closed communications, now there are the airplane, the Internet, the cellphone, Skype, social media, and a steady proliferation of new means to meet and to share ideas. A history of such interactions during the past fifteen years has provided a major element in the momentum that has produced the present meeting. The gradual *imborghesimento* of Italian America, and in Italy the growing recognition that immigration is itself a progressively opening circuit—these are social realities that have combined to produce among scholars a widespread recognition that the moment is propitious for such a meeting.

2. *Antiquated Models of Ideology.*

Students of postcolonialism know that the systematics of colonialism do not disappear in a single day or, in some aspects, ever at all. Resistance to immigration is strong in many countries, among them both the United States and Italy. Old attachments to antiquated models of social stability continue to exercise a hypnotic power over many citizens.

These attachments continue to be worrisome and to require attention. Sunday morning, Martino Marazzi told me that one of his *laureandi* at the University of Milano had written a thesis on the novelist Garibaldi LaPolla. The other professor assigned to the student's defense refused to read this thesis, even the abstract of the thesis, on the grounds that immigrants are no fit subject for literature. This *rifiuto* arises not from the thirteenth century but from last month.

Last year, I was speaking to class of *laureandi* in Rome about a work of Italian American writing. One student suggested that he and his classmates had no need to concern themselves with this literature. "Are you suggesting that the *emigrati* were inferior persons?" I asked. "Of course," he replied. "Otherwise, they would never have left."

3. *Repression of New Ideas.*

The brutal messages that became a daily part of the life of the Congolese-Italian Cécile Kyenge when she was Italy's minister of integration furnish a good example of repression in motion. Even the Vice-President of the Italian Senate Calderoli publicly referred to her in flagrantly racist terms. Kyenge's support of a plan to grant citizenship to children of immigrants who were born on Italian soil met serious resistance. The writings of the *clandestini* need to be published, to be read, to be discussed.

4. *Underfunding*

Austerity programs in both Europe and the United States have made it difficult, and often impossible, to develop new ways of assisting the growth of immigrant cultures in these countries.

Conclusion

These are only a few of the many obvious resistances that face us. Let me add that, if I had no hope, I'd have stayed home. But it is important to assess things at their proper weight and to remind ourselves that literature is a basic weapon in the social armamentarium of outsiders. As such, it cannot help challenging prejudices and shedding light on uncomfortable realities. It cannot help meeting resistance. Italian American literature can, of course, avoid such resistance by re-inscribing colonial attitudes and ideologies forever. But, no matter what we do, literature is always a suspect. It has the power and the habit of telling uncomfortable truths. Only by doing so can it thrive, can it make itself worthy of readers outside its places of origin. When we leave this place and go the airport, someone will be waiting there to empty our bags and look through what we have been reading and writing. "Books!" this person will exclaim. "Why so many books?"

Creating Italian American Studies Programs

Fred Gardaphé
Queens College, CUNY

Italian American studies probably began the moment the first Italian immigrant wondered to him- or herself: "What the hell am I doing here?" Until recently knowing the date and time of that precise moment never mattered. Since Italian American studies were not taken seriously enough, even by some of its practitioners, to warrant historization, the moment of its birth has never been a concern. Its parents, both American and Italian studies had abandoned the child at birth, so it doesn't even know it own birthday. And this would remain true as long as Italians were the objects of, and not the agents of, studies in the academy.

Formal Italian American studies actually begin when the scholar trained in the U.S. applied a disciplinary focus to cultural productions of Americans of Italian descent. However, Italian American Studies became realized as a field of study when scholars turned the interpretative gaze back on their own and earlier work. Some of these early scholars include: Helen Barolini, Patrick Gallo, Richard Gambino, Rose Basile Green, Olga Peragallo, Rudolph Vecoli, and Robert Viscusi. Italian American Studies became further legitimized when institutions began developing programs of study.

Without scholarly societies or formal programs inside institutions, American intellectuals intent on developing Italian American studies had to do so independently, and more often than not their work was not considered "real work." At least two generations of Italian American scholars so far could hardly have taught a course dedicated to the study of Italian Americans. During the 1960s and 1970s, Italian American intellectuals begin producing books based on studies of their own culture. Two, which characterize best Italian American studies during this period are Richard Gambino's *Blood of My Blood*, and Patrick Gallo's *Ethnic Alienation: The Italian Americans*. Only now are these books being read seriously and critiqued properly.

From: *Transcending Borders, Bridging Gaps* (Calandra Institute, 2015)

A key stage in the "risorgimento" of Italian American studies occurred in 1967 through the founding of the American Italian Historical Association. The association dedicated its second annual conference to the Italian American novel. It is through that association that some of Italian Americana's best literary criticism has come to be known.

Unlike the development of many other ethnic and gender studies programs, those that have emerged in Italian American studies, did not result from direct, popular political actions. The beneficiary of earlier the social protest movements that produced those Studies program in academia, Italian American Studies developed in earnest long after programs in African-American and Women's studies. More discrete and individualized work was conducted to create the earliest efforts in Italian American studies and political activity has only become a recent strategy in advocating its development. The most celebrated case of political action surrounded the John D. Calandra Italian American Institute of the City University of New York system. After years of operating as a research and career counseling center, the Calandra Institute, fortified by a study conducted by the above-mentioned Richard Gambino, a pioneer in the field of Italian American studies, received permanent funding after a winning the 1992 Scelsa vs. CUNY lawsuit. A settlement reached in 1994 granted the Institute university-wide research status, provided permanent funding for the Calandra Institute, which fosters higher education for Italian Americans, and attached a Distinguished Professorship to the Institute through Queens College—first occupied by late Dr. Philip Cannistraro, from 1996 until his death in 2005.

Under the direction of Dr. Philip Cannistraro, the first Distinguished Professor of Italian American studies, the curriculum was redesigned into an interdisciplinary approach in 2000. Its philosophy is that Italian history and culture are essential to understanding the Italian presence in American society. The program offers courses in three broad areas: cultural studies (literature, film studies, Italian language, art, and music), The Social and Political Heritage (history, political science, sociology, and ethnic studies), and language studies (all levels of Italian language). The program works closely with the John D. Calandra Italian American Institute now headed by Dr. Anthony Julian Tamburri.

Over the years, many institutions have offered individual courses in Italian American studies. One of the leading locations is Nassau Community

College in Long Island, New York, which through the leadership of Dr. Salvatore LaGumina and Dr. Joseph Varacalli established a Center for Italian American Studies. Another center was established by Brooklyn College Center for Italian American Studies that sponsors research projects, conferences and cultural events. Among its services are workshops in counseling and training.

In the mid-1980s Dr. Mario Mignone, then Chair of the Department of French and Italian at SUNY-Stony Brook, developed a minor in Italian American Studies that has since grown into the leading undergraduate Italian American Studies program in the United States. Professor Mignone, who is founder and director of the university's Center for Italian Studies, created the academic program and in 1998 hired Dr. Fred Gardaphé to direct it. A year later, the university hired Dr. Mary Jo Bona as well. In 2000, Stony Brook University, in partnership with UNICO-National directed by Frank Cannata and Joseph Coccia, who have served as chairs of the UNICO fundraising committee, launched a campaign to raise 1.5 million dollars to create an endowed professorship in Italian American Studies. The Alfonse M. D'Amato Chair of Italian and Italian American Studies was filled six years ago with the appointment of Dr. Peter Carravetta. The Stony Brook program offers a minor and serves over 2,000 students per year through its course offerings.

Hofstra University added to Italian American studies programs in 2008 through its appointment of Dr. Pellegrino D'Acierno as the Queensboro UNICO endowed professorship in Italian American studies; Professor Stanislao Pugliese is the current holder of that chair.

The only university in the United States currently offering a major in Italian American studies is Hebert Lehman College, of the CUNY system. The program was led by Dr. Anthony LaRuffa until his recent retirement. Seton Hall University has the Joseph M. and Geraldine C. Motta Chair of Italian studies launched in partnership with UNICO National in 1998. Dr. William Connell directs this program of Italian studies that includes a course on Italian American history.

At John Carroll University, near Cleveland, The Bishop Anthony M. Pilla Program in Italian American Studies was established with the support of the Northern Ohio Italian American (NOIA) Foundation. This undergraduate program, directed by Dr. Santa Casciani, is named for the bishop of the Diocese of Cleveland and works to recognize and salute the contributions of Italians and Italian Americans to the history and culture of the United States.

Montclair State University in New Jersey is the home of the Joseph and Elda Coccia Institute for the Italian Experience in America that fosters the development of Italian American Studies at the university where there is a strong series of undergraduate courses in Italian American studies. Three years ago, the university hired Teresa Fiore as the Inserra Chair of Italian and Italian American Studies.

In California, California State Universities at Chico, Long Beach, and Northridge all have developed Italian American Studies programs. Eugenio Frongia taught everything from Dante to the Renaissance to film to Italian American history; Flavio Orsitto now continues that tradition. At California State Long Beach, Clorinda Donato holds the George L. Graziadio Chair, and directs the Center for Italian Studies. This is another UNICO National fundraising effort.[1] In the 2001-2002 school year, New York University launched a rotating chair in Italian American studies that was endowed by the Tiro al Segno Organization of New York. Dr. Josephine Gattuso Hendin of the English Department at NYU served as the first chair and teaches a course in Italian American literature in those semesters when the chair is not filled.

While there is still no formal program leading to a doctorate in Italian American Studies, Professors Fred Gardaphé and Anthony Julian Tamburri have developed graduate courses in the field at Queens College through the Master of Liberal Arts and Italian Master's Degree programs. For over twenty-five years, Professors Mary Jo Bona, Fred Gardaphé, and Anthony Julian Tamburri have directed and served on dissertation committees for students in the U.S. and Italy. They have also taught graduate and undergraduate courses at Purdue University, Columbia College-Chicago, Florida Atlantic and Stony Brook Universities, enabling a new generation of scholars to develop in the growing field. Recently, Gardaphé and Tamburri have taught Italian American studies at the University of Perugia and the University of Calabria, where together with Professors Margherita Ganeri and Marta Petrusewicz, they have created a seminar in

[1] As this publication goes to press, Cal State LB has announced a new MA Program in Italian Studies for Fall 2014; an Italian-American component will be part of that degree.

Italian American studies that is required for all graduate students in modern and contemporary Italian literature.

The inclusion of Italian American Studies at more institutions of higher education will depend on a number of factors. Colleges and universities are the major repositories for learning. With the explosion of information in our society there much competition for what gets researched and taught. How can Italian American culture (spanning just 200 years and including a small percentage of the population of the U.S.) find a place in this chaos?

It is a time-honored practice for wealthy individuals, motivated groups, industries, and the government to influence university research and teaching by donating large sums of money to create endowed professorships dedicated to a field of special interest to the donor. For example, a million dollars donated as an endowment (never to be spent), at a 5% dividend, would generate $50,000 per year. That $50,000, in turn, would be used by the university independently to hire personnel to carry on the research and teaching of Italian American Studies in perpetuity. At least one person could research, write, and teach the next generation of scholars who could carry on the process FOREVER. In addition to money, though, we need understanding, moral support by the larger community, and patronage by the younger generation of Italian American students. The most recent development in fundraising comes out of Chicago, where Loyola University has launched a campaign to endow a Chair in Italian American Studies.

Today work under the name of Italian American Studies is proliferating. Publications such *as Voices in Italian Americana*, *Italian Americana*, *The Italian American Review*, *Fra Noi*, *Primo*, and the most recent addition of *i-Italy.org* have further legitimated the development of programs of study. Key scholars in disciplines such as English, History, and Cultural Studies and in many organizations such as the Italian American Studies Association (formerly American Italian Historical Association), the Modern Language Association, the Society for the Study of Multi-Ethnic Literature of the United States (a.k.a., MELUS), Malìa: A Collective of Italian American Women, the American Association of Teachers of Italian (AATI), and the American Association of Italian Studies, have worked with the Italian American communities around the country to institutionalize Italian American Studies.

Elemental Bibliography

Barolini, Helen. *The Dream Book: An Anthology of Writings by Italian American Women*. New York: Schoken, 1985.

Basile Green, Rose. *The Italian-American Novel: A Documentation of the Interaction between Two Cultures*. Madison NJ: Fairleigh Dickinson UP, 1974.

Bona, Mary Jo, ed. *The Voices We Carry: Recent Italian American Women's Fiction*. Toronto: Guernica Editions, 2006 2nd edition.

D'Acierno, Pellegrino, ed. *The Italian American Heritage*. New York: Garland, 1999.

Gallo, Patrick. *Ethnic Alienation: The Italian-Americans*. Madison, NJ: Fairleigh Dickinson University Press, 1974.

Gambino, Richard. *Blood of My Blood*. New York: Anchor, 1975.

Gardaphé, Fred. "Creating a Program in Italian American Studies." In *Teaching Italian American Literature, Film, and Popular Culture*. Edvige Giunta and Kathleen McCormick, eds. New York: Modern Language Association, 2010. 79-83.

Giunta, Edvige and Kathleen McCormick, eds. *Teaching Italian American Literature, Film, and Popular Culture*. New York: Modern Language Association, 2010.

LaGumina, Salvatore. *WOP: A Documentary History of Anti-Italian Discrimination*. Toronto: Guernica, 1999; first published in 1973.

LaGumina, Salvatore J., Frank J. Cavaioli, Salvatore Primeggia and Joseph A. Varacalli, eds. *The Italian American Experience: An Encyclopedia*. New York: Routledge, 1999.

Peragallo, Olga. *Italian-American Authors and Their Contribution to American Literature*. New York: S. F. Vanni, 1949.

Tamburri, Anthony Julian, Paolo A. Giordano, and Fred L. Gardaphé, eds. *From The Margin. Writings in Italian Americana*. West Lafayette IN: Purdue UP, 1991, 2nd ed. 2000.

Vecoli, Rudolph J. "Contadini in Chicago: A Critique of The Uprooted," *Journal of American History* 5 (December 1964): 404–17.

Viscusi, Robert. "*De vulgari eloquentia*. An Approach to the Language of Italian American Fiction," *Yale Italian Studies*, 1.3 (1981): 21-38.

Amicus curiae

Djelal Kadir
Penn State University

A hyphen is a dash convinced it doesn't have far to go. A slash is a slanted mirror persuaded of its own transparency and permeability. Both are signs of turbulent psychohistories and their enduring traumas. Many a hyphen's hope has been dashed on the sudden realization that the longest distance between two points is a straight line, and just as many a slash has shattered and burned in the incandescence of the illusion that history can be leapfrogged like an ocean between continents. Terminally indeterminable, the historical trajectory of those destined to dash across the hyphen or traverse the specter of the slash find themselves trapped in perpetuity between ghosts of a *terminus a quo* and the no less spectral hopes of a *terminus ad quem.* The memory of the first and the illusions of the latter invariably complicate the landscape of the present. And one of the most graphic dramatizations of this predicament is the Taviani Brothers' 1984 film *Kaos,* based on tales of Luigi Pirandello. Both past and future exist in inverse ratio to the possibilities of the moment, with *now* proportionally diminishing in relation to the persistence of *then,* whether *then* is *a quo* or *ad quem*—an unforgettable starting line or a yearned destination. Memory and desire tend to squeeze out the middle term. By reckonings of prosody and logic, such existence cannot be anything but enthymemic, like the syllogism whose middle third term is congenitally compromised. In this algorithm, life can only be lived as a compromised concession; anything else is a pretense straining to assuage the tenuous status of reality

This is my brief, an *amicus* brief in terms of canonical and civil law and the sacred rules of friendship. It adheres closely to the indispensable condition of life lived as an act of faith when historical circumstances permit no alternative. The requisite condition is as old as any human communion, and just as fragile. Greek antiquity referred to it as *philía,* and the Roman Church anointed the term in the Greek Vulgate. It is a labor of love, an articulation that binds in filial and affiliative commitment. In his most re-

From: *Transcending Borders, Bridging Gaps* (Calandra Institute, 2015)

cent book, Anthony Tamburri earnestly advocates for a recuperation of the meaning and acts of philanthropy as more than patronage. My philanthropy has always been in the spirit of *philía*, and my relationship to this *curia* has always been defined by *philía*'s *amicitia,* hence my *amicus* brief.

Dashing across the field of Italian American studies, as one must, lest one get slashed in empathy and burnt by the affective identification that redounds to one's own migrant traumas, one thing is very clear: Italian American studies is markedly different when studied by Italian Americans than, say, by Italians or Americans. And that is why it is important that Italian American Studies be the studious focus of all. Those engaged in this endeavor comprise a trinity: Italian, American, and Italian American. Being none of the above, except contingently, it becomes clear to me that the triangulation of the three poses a contradiction: the contradiction being that, in their imbrications, all three are and are not each other. A philosophically paradoxical American himself, William James taught that when we come to a contradiction our best recourse is to make a distinction, something James' school of American Pragmatism learned from the incongruous predicaments of a German-Italian by the name of Nicolas of Cusa and his paradoxical 1440 treatise called *De Docta Ignorantia.* I don't know much about being Italian or American, and even less about being Italian American. And when I became an Americanist I did so on the word of Voltaire, "Quand on écrit l'histoire, il faut n'être d'aucun pays" ("When writing history, one must not be of any country"). In his early modernity Enlightenment, Voltaire glimpsed the perils of auto-history and self-writing. What he could not have foreseen are the no-less perilous predicaments we have come to appreciate in our late modernity, namely, the belated realization that writing others, or writing what one is not, might not be any less hazardous than writing oneself. We have since also learned from anthropological discourse that the emic self-presentation is no less parlous than the etic representation of a given culture from the outside.

It was the paradox of these contesting realizations that served as the impetus for convening two dozen Americanists at Villa Serbelloni in May of 2000 to interrogate the slippage from Voltaire's monitory injunction and the falling into an unalloyed solipsism that was American cultural studies by the end of the twentieth century, a self-absorbed spectralization that imploded into the identity politics of the era, of which *American*

American studies continues to be an egregiously unreconstructed instance. The result of that contentious conversation at this *locus amoenus* was the founding of the International American Studies Association, an earnest attempt to snatch American studies back from self-blinding invagination even as the country was on the verge of a new era of bellicose self-assertiveness and another iteration of its perennial exceptionalist identitarianism on a global scale, thus matching its re-tractive cultural implosion with the violence of an outward explosion that characterizes America's current defensive-aggressive realpolitik. The culture wars of the final decade of the last century in U.S. political life and social discourse thus passed into the war culture that ushered in the twenty-first century. Among the baleful consequences of that transition has been the throttling of civic discourse and the fraying of political gains achieved by the diverse cultural threads that weave the fabric of American society and history. A turn that could perhaps partially explain Anthony Tamburri's recent observation to the effect that "an organization that is the American Studies Association engages in a type of hegemony that *de facto* discounts any validity to Italian Americana as a valid field of study" (10). The centrifugal projection of U.S. hyper-power on a planetary scale in the first decade and a half of the new century has its mirrored introjection in the fury of a centripetal vortex that spins difference, diversity, and heterodox identities into the conformity and monotone of American triumphalism and its righteous shrillness in what passes for public discourse. The only alternative to that vociferation appears to be the brooding silence of those who know better but can find no public space for living by the courage of their convictions, or are not even able to find a margin of safety for letting on that they possess either courage or convictions.

American studies in this national echo chamber becomes a monaural hum, with the polyvocity of multicultural counterpoint, dissonance, and harmonics absorbed into a homogeneous murmur of white noise, in the well-known phrase of an Italian American writer. In its perennial penchant for echoing the national chorus it purportedly scrutinizes, parses, and interrogates, American studies in the USA and its satellites has spun into what it calls the "transnational turn," an on-cue turning away from the interactive and mutual reciprocity of international and inter-cultural conversation and toward pugnaciously transitive action, a turn that reflects the projective trajectory of U.S. American power and transnational monopoly capital that, once again, has found its most profitable optimization in that national turn from the contestatory culture wars of the twentieth century to the virulent war culture of the first decade of the twenty first. Under today's historical circumstances, like all intellectual endeavors and cultural discourses, American studies that are more than American, however tendentious that designation may be, are only likely to find an environment conducive to their calling and apposite to their survival in proportion to the degree that their métier conforms to what drives the national cause as defined by those in a position to define it. The engine that drives the national American cause and its manufactured consensus is, more than ever, capital profit and, as noted already, the most profitable enterprise has been deemed, once again, to be war, a phenomenon that has always lived up to its historically confirmed definition as killing for profit.

Italian American studies is more than American studies, but it is not a war party discourse. In fact, its genesis as a cultural formation is in good measure a consequence of the disasters of war and its traumatic historical repercussions that, to a large degree, led to the Italian diaspora that became Italian American. And Italian America today finds itself downwind of a public discourse that resonates with eerie familiarity in a war-smitten epoch that has declared its own destiny as one of perpetual war: "And above all [. . .] the more it considers and observes quite apart from political considerations of the moment, believes neither in the possibility nor the utility of perpetual peace. . . War alone brings up to its highest tension all human energy and puts the stamp of nobility upon the people who have the courage to meet it" (qtd in Smedley D. Butler, *War Is A Racket:* http://www.ratical.org/ratville/CAH/war isaracket.pdf). "It" in this case is Fascism and the voice is Il Duce's. Premier Mussolini is speaking in 1935, paradoxically enough, in "International Conciliation," a publication of the Carnegie Endowment for International Peace.

Which is to say that Italian American studies endures the repercussions of a cultural and political environment in which it has been embedded and that is defining of its historic and historical role. This is the environment it seeks to transcend and the complex in which it seeks to build bridges. Transcendence, whether beyond circumstance, as Anthony Tamburri would have it, or beyond identity, as Peter Carravetta promises to explain, has always proved a rather intricate matter; and bridge building has always been a highly challenging engineering feat. Transcendence and bridging, the declared admirable goals of this august occasion, are an intriguing combination and very much a paradoxical crossroads where, as William James cautioned, distinction becomes indispensable. A master of American Transcendentalism, Ralph Waldo Emerson noted that something happens to eternity any time we pass the time of day. Which is to say that if eternity itself is susceptible to the happenstance of life's accidents, historical permutations are no less subject to the vicissitudes of contingency. The hazards of transcendence, then, would be prone to strip any subject agency of any immunity from the fortuitous circumstances of the environment it would seek to transcend. In fact, those fortuities historically prove to be defining both of the desiring subject and its transcendental desiderata, demonstrating yet again that human identity, individual or collective, is inexorably circumscribed by the historical environment it seeks to define and transcend, whether it seeks to do so across bridges, or by gravity-defying levitation.

The historical record of Italian American studies in this regard has been amply documented, most ably by a number of lucid and articulate participant observers in the field sitting around this table. And your admirable efforts make something perfectly clear, namely, that Italian American studies as scholarly and pedagogical discourse, on the one hand, and as the life-world of Italian Americans and their history, on the other, are two separate phenomena, at times overlapping, as in the distinguished persons of some here, but distinct, nonetheless, as exemplified by a number of specialists of Italian American studies who happen not to be Italian Americans. The identity politics of America's recent multiculturalist engagements have tended to blur, and often devalue distinctions between those doing the studying and those being studied by cultural or ethno-racial studies. Voltaire's admonition about writing a people's history should be a salutary reminder in this regard, as should the reminder, in 1976, by historiographer Raphael Samuel of Ruskin College, Oxford: "history is too important to be left just to the professional historians." (http://www.history.ac.uk/makinghistory/resources/articles/HWJ.html) It may be apt to extrapolate from Samuel's apothegm that Italian American studies is significant enough to merit a perennial place across the curriculum and at a diversity of institutional and disciplinary contexts within educational institutions. The question then becomes, how does that panoply of institutional foci trained on Italian American culture relate to the ethnic identity of its object of study? The question takes on a certain urgency in the current fiscal dynamics of educational and cultural institutions at a time when public and state formations are being systematically privatized and become ever more reliant on underwriting that is neither legislatively appropriated, nor predictably annualized in governmental and state budgets of educational institutions. If Italian American studies must rely on the munificence of private Italian American patronage, whether as academic curriculum or as documentary archive, or as focus of scholarly research, how do Italian American studies avoid becoming an exclusive Italian American concern, or a green-lined ghetto in which Italian American studies caters to Italian Americans through Italian American underwriting, with occasional strategic outreach to other demographics?

These are questions that pertain to all American studies in America and outside of America, wherever America is studied, whether they are African American studies, Latino American studies, Native American studies, or Asian American studies, *inter alios*. It is historically important to keep in mind that the relationship among these studious spheres is not strictly analogical, or simply parallel, but there is something repercussive and causal in their imbricated co-existence. The history of America moots the viability of anything that claims to be simply "American Studies," despite the proprietary clamoring of the American Studies Association (ASA) that as a self-fashioned axial association is still more prone to associate with itself as solipsistic construct convinced of its own amalgam as radial axis, rather than embracing the multiple and variegated congeries that constitutes a polymorphous phenomenon called America. And while the last quarter of the twentieth century disproved the notion of an alembicated amalgam, or the oft-idealized *e pluribus unum*, in terms of the frequently invoked lyrical idyll of Virgil, the institutional formations that cultivated that desideratum have yet to reconcile themselves to the Virgilian idyll's historical fatuity. This amounts to a denial of historical disconfirmation that has undermined the possibility of a post-culture-wars rapprochement among the multiplicity of American studies that carry a modifier before "American." The decimation of the social compact, of the public sphere, and of civic consensus in America has led to a social Darwinism that has pockmarked the first decade and a half of the new century. This, in turn, has exacerbated the politics of social fragmentation inherited from the culture wars, and cultural studies are no less atomized now than the sundry cultures that pertain to them. The institutional contexts such as universities, colleges, civic organizations, heritage societies where the multiplicity of ethnic, racial, or cultural studies might converge into productive synergies find themselves straining for their individual and independent survival, much less serving as interdependent sites that nurture social formations and institutional discourses, especially if those institutional formations do not happen to carry ready cash value or are not fungible enough to be leveraged for patronage revenue.

One could make the claim that our being here belies the reality of this dire predicament. But our stated mission to transcend these circumstances and to breach the gaps or chasms that oblige Italian American studies foci to operate as superannuated sites in isolation simply confirms the recognition by institutions such as the Rockefeller Foundation, the John D. Calandra Italian American Institute, and the Institute for International Education supporting our colloquy of the direness of the situation for cultural studies of all ethnicities. The question for us, implicit in the support of this gathering, is, are we capable of imagining ways that can compensate for the nine in ten that have been decimated in the realignment of social and political agenda, the nine in ten in fiscal resources that have been shifted to the ever-fewer few in a historically unprecedented pace of redistribution of public wealth and the transformation of federal and state governments into concessioners of the public commonweal turned over to plutocratic structures? How, in other words, do we ameliorate the structural violence that has transformed public institutions into mercenary franchise of private interests? And how does Italian American studies, like all other American studies that carry a modifier before American, fit into and survive this predicament? One concrete answer to this question whose urgency gathers us here could well be the institutional formation that was born at this auspicious Italian location nearly a decade and a half ago, namely, the International American Studies Association, currently under an Italian presidency in the distinguished person of our colleague Giorgio Mariani, an organization whose Italian membership happens to be the largest of any other country among the more than three dozen countries from around the world that comprise the association. IASA, *mirabile dictu,* happens to be the pivotal point where Italian, American, and Italian American institutional formations and critical discourses converge. And the kind of synergy that this convergence promises is precisely one of the strongest

founding principles and the raison d'être of the International American Studies Association, a fact to which Giorgio and our esteemed colleague Donatella Izzo, another current member of IASA's Executive Council around this table, could attest.

The term "Italian" at this historical juncture is no longer limited to populations in Italy and in the United States of America. With an Italian diaspora of over 60 million people around the planet, and with the term America no longer understood as referring exclusively to the United States but extending to a bi-continental hemisphere with thirty-five countries and fifteen territories, the international dimensions and discursive resonance of the binomial "Italian American" can hardly be overlooked. With both "Italian" and "American" denoting a demographic that is global, the International American Studies Association offers a convergent cartography that is congruent with the globality of what Italian American means in the twenty first century. The recent anthology of Italian poetry by more than seventy Italian-language poets from eleven distinct areas of the world—I am referring to the 2014 Fordham University Press volume titled *Poets of the Italian Diaspora: A Bilingual Anthology* and edited by Luigi Bonaffini and Joseph Periccone—certainly points the way to an internationally expanded understanding of the term Italian. And the endorsement and promotion of this publication by the John D. Calandra Italian American Institute of New York may well mean the mapping onto an understanding of what the terms Italian, American, and Italian American as international phenomena mean. Our gathering here may not be an insignificant event in this global context and its emergent international ramifications. At this juncture, we seem to be walking into a morphing discursive and cultural landscape haunted by perennial and often contestatory histories of the autochthonous, the dialectal, the vernacular, the national, and the cosmopolitan, all in a convergent, yet asynchronous simultaneity that embraces the multiple signification of the term Italian American today.

A Public Space for Italian American Studies
The John D. Calandra Italian American Institute

Joseph Sciorra
John D. Calandra Italian American Institute, Queens College, CUNY

On March 12, 2012, the John D. Calandra Italian American Institute screened Abel Ferrrara's *Mulberry St.* (2009, 87 mins) as part of its "Documented Italians" film and video series. The film details preparations for the annual San Gennaro *festa* in New York City's Little Italy. Ferrara explains in the film that the street feast "brings all the characters out," as he introduces viewers to individuals like Butchie the Hat, Cha Cha, Joey Cigar, Baby John, and other local nicknamed personalities who reminisce about the feast in the time before Mayor Rudolph Giuliani intervened to rid the event of organized crime. *Mulberry St.*, with its indecorous characters, recurrent profanity, and nonlinear narrative, is neither a conventional documentary nor an attempt at ethnic boosterism.

The film elicited a wide range of reactions from the audience, an eclectic mix of scholars and the general public. One man found the film to be an honest portrayal of the type of neighborhood denizens he grew up with in Brooklyn. "I lost close people to the streets; thankfully, my daughters don't know about that life," he said during the post-screening Q&A with the director. Another audience member told Ferrara, "The people in that film are a bunch of gavones, and you're the king of gavones!" She concluded by telling Ferrara bluntly that he should burn his film. This exchange, while passionate at times, eventually led to a more tempered conversation about the role of documentary films, a director's point of view, the history of Italian Americans in New York City, and cinematic depictions of that group.

This type of discourse is at the heart of the Calandra Institute's commitment to disseminating in the public sphere recent scholarship and creative work pertaining to the history and culture of Italian Americans and the larger Italian diaspora. As Queens College/City University of New York's research institute for Italian American studies, the Calandra Institute operates dynamically on various fronts to conduct and promote rigor-

ous interdisciplinary inquiry. As we seek to expand the reach of Italian American studies, as part of the Italian American Studies Network formed in Bellagio, we recognize how public fora featuring scholarly inquiry are indispensable for advancing its objectives. The Calandra Institute's pioneering and robust public programing serves as a model for such work.

The Calandra Institute came into being in 1979, but it was not until 1997 that it made public programming a mainstay of its activities. It was in that year that historian Philip V. Cannistraro was appointed Distinguished Professor of Italian American Studies at Queens College, a position closely affiliated with the Institute. His vision was for a "new Calandra," one that involved an ongoing series of lectures, symposia, and other public programs. It was understood that one of the Institute's core missions—that of serving Italian-American students at the City University of New York—needed to be re-examined as that population and its difficulties (e.g., significant high-school dropout rates) diminished. The shift to establishing a public space for the expanding work of Italian American-studies scholars was deemed an important next step in strengthening the Institute's other priority, that of promoting understanding and research about Italian Americans.

Given his academic interests as a historian of Italian fascism and antifascism, Cannistraro organized the two-day symposium "The Lost World of Italian American Radicalism" in 1997. He followed that successful event by curating the exhibition "The Italians of New York" at the New-York Historical Society (1999–2000), a broad overview (including lectures and presentations) documenting Italian Americans' influence in the city's economic, political, and cultural life. These two projects set the course for the Institute's work reaching beyond the ivory tower.

In 1999, a new division of "Academic and Cultural Programs" was created at Calandra to formalize this work, and I was hired to lead it. My background as an academically trained folklorist researching and presenting community-based, vernacular artists vis-à-vis public institutions such as historical societies, museums, and nonprofit organizations, was well-suited for developing Cannistraro's new initiative. Together he and I collaborated on the monthly "Seminar Series in Italian American Studies" (which I renamed in Cannistraro's memory following his death in 2005), a forum where scholars present their current research; and in 2000, we organized our first symposium, "Religion and Spirituality in Italian American

Life." We soon developed an array of all-day symposia, roundtable discussions, and other presentations taking place throughout the academic year. In time, a number of these programs have resulted in refereed publications such as *The Lost World of Italian American Radicalism: Politics, Labor, and Culture* (2003), edited by Philip V. Cannistraro and Gerald Meyer, and *Embroidered Stories: Interpreting Women's Domestic Needlework from the Italian Diaspora* (2014), which Edvige Giunta and I co-edited.

After Philip Cannistraro's death, I took the lead in public programming at the Institute, establishing two new series: "Writers Read," which offers opportunities for contemporary poets, novelists, playwrights, and memoirists to read and discuss their published works before an audience; and "Documented Italians," a series dedicated to screening independent documentary films and videos that, for the most part, have limited access to commercial theaters and are rarely seen.

Notwithstanding the success, popularity, and significance of these programs, the infrastructure for a complete and proper response to them, including provision for remuneration of the presenters, was not yet in place at the Institute. It was with the appointment of Anthony Tamburri as dean of the Institute that public programming became recognized as a major component of the Institute's activities. In addition to organizing programs on his own, Tamburri earmarked funding for speakers and hired new staff—Rosangela Briscese, in particular, as coordinator for Academic and Cultural Programs—to formalize and strengthen the Institute's commitment to this crucial work.

Shortly after Dean Tamburri's arrival the Institute inaugurated its first annual conference, on the theme of "Italians in the Americas," in 2008. Every year, a small group of staff members conceive, develop, and produce a two-day annual conference around a new theme that draws an international consortium of academics. With each successive year, the number and geographic scope of the papers increase. The 2014 conference "MAFIAs: Realities and Representations of Organized Crime" was so large and of such broad import that it was convened in partnership with CUNY's John Jay College of Criminal Justice. Presenters to these gatherings have gone on to submit their articles for publication in the Institute's social science and cultural studies journal *Italian American Review*.

The Calandra Institute's public presence is also strongly felt on the Internet. Facebook and Twitter are more than merely effective means of

publicizing events at the Institute's midtown Manhattan office; they are also vehicles for disseminating and discussing new publications, films, and news items from across the globe. Live-streaming (and subsequent archiving) of presenters at the annual conferences, as well as posting the Institute's television program *Italics* on YouTube, has resulted in the creation of a valuable online library that is open and available to all. In addition, Tamburri and I are invited bloggers at i-Italy.org where we write about various and sundry issues concerning Italian Americana.

The Institute's public programming is predicated on the notion that the Italian-American "experience" is anything but singular. Italian-American lives, histories, and cultures are diverse and multifaceted, increasingly open to new interpretations and revisions. The Institute invites scholars and artists who have presented an encyclopedic range of germane topics, from classic Neapolitan songs to punk music; Catholic ex-voto paintings to non-representational sculpture; mountain *zampognari* (bagpipers) to suburban Guidos; and fascists in Argentina to anarchists in Paterson, New Jersey. These social, cultural, and political persuasions constitute the varied parts of the larger story of the Italian diaspora. Our programs offer provocative and sometimes disconcerting readings of Italian-American experiences.

Equally important in the Institute's programming is the opportunity to offer alternatives to nostalgic perceptions of immigration, family life, notions of community, and the more general feel-good ethnic pride that circulate in the popular media and are promoted to a large degree by mainstream membership voluntary associations. As I have written elsewhere,

> Italian Americans have developed a mythic narrative that chronicles their triumph over harrowing deprivation, economic exploitation, and ethnic discrimination, as well as their ascent into middle- and upper-middle-class success, troubled only by continued depictions of the mafia in cinema and television. This uncritical and linear account of self-resolve, family cohesion, and religious conviction ending in the boardrooms and suburbia of white America involves a significant amount of memory loss and obfuscation of the historical record (2004, 459).

Scholars are critiquing and dismantling the flag-waving triumphalism and pedestrian assumptions that emerged out of the 1970s white ethnic movement. Artists too challenge conventional notions about cultural politics and Italian-American identity through the themes of their work. By including their perspectives as part of the Institute's programs, intellectual space is made available for creative engagement with identity formation in various Italian diasporic settings.

This vision of public scholarship has not been embraced by all. Negative reactions have been voiced in the digital sphere via email blasts and blog posts. For example, several self-appointed ethnic spokespeople called for a boycott of the all-day colloquium "Guido: An Italian-American Youth Style" (see Airos and Cappelli, 2011, and "Guido: An Italian-American Youth Style"). After the Call for Papers for the "MAFIAs" conference was circulated online on July 9, 2013, two Italian studies professors (whom I have chosen not to mention by name) at Stony Brook University initiated a condemnation of the international event via email, stating that it was "a cultural tragedy" and "for those of us teaching Italian language and courses relating to Italian culture, it is absurd and completely counterproductive to promote negative images of Italians and Italian Americans" (personal communication, July 10, 2013). Yet, anthropologist Jane Schneider (The Graduate Center, CUNY) and sociologist Peter Schneider (Fordham University), both of whom participated in the conference, came to a different conclusion:

> The Calandra Institute should be congratulated for imagining and organizing a remarkably productive conference on mafias and their representations. For a very long time, attention to mafias flourished in popular culture and the mass media but received less attention in academia, save for a small number of specialized criminologists. ... As an interdisciplinary endeavor, the Calandra Institute conference took a big step toward challenging these misconceptions. Both historians and social scientists analyzed mafias outside as well as inside the United States and Italy. Scholars of film and literature drew attention to recent transformations in the ways popular culture represents mafiosi, their practices, and values. Perhaps most important, the conference also included writers and journalists who have studied anti-mafia processes, both in the criminal justice sector and among committed citizens. That mafias, where they flourish, coexist with and provoke anti-mafia movements is a memorable takeaway from the conference. (2014, 4. See also Cappelli 2014, 10-12 and Sciorra 2014)

The impact of the Institute's public programs is far-reaching. For scholars and artists, it provides a vehicle for making their work known, not only in the face-to-face contacts with audience members but also through the simple online dissemination of their work vis-à-vis the announcement of the events. Most importantly, little-known subject matter is made more accessible to a wider audience of people who are seeking knowledge about Italian-American history and culture that is all too often not readily available or all but invisible in the mainstream media.[1] In this way, individuals who regularly attend events have commented on learning about and enjoying presentations on such diverse topics as New York City architect Rosario Candela; self-taught artist Silvio Barile of Michigan; Sicilian-American fishermen in Gloucester, Massachusetts; and Italian-Irish fish and chip-shop owners in Dublin, Ireland. This imparting of knowledge is immeasurable and it serves to create an ever-expanding community of interested individuals learning about Italian American studies.

We are witnessing a worldwide proliferation of stimulating research on Italian-American history and culture. For more than fifteen years, the John D. Calandra Italian American Institute has provided the public—gratis—with a forum for scholars, authors, visual artists, and filmmakers to present their work in a rich and diverse array of programming. It is this work that feeds and sustains the free flow of ideas at the heart of the Institute's ongoing mission of supporting Italian American studies.

[1] Profiles of audience members are published in the Institute's newsletter *Il Bollettino*, which can be found online at http://qcpages.qc.cuny.edu/calandra/il-bollettino.

Works Cited

Airos, Letizia, and Ottorino Cappelli, eds. 2011. *Guido: Italian/American Youth and Identity Politics*. New York: Bordighera Press.

Cappelli, Ottorino. 2014. "Investigating Mafia(s) on a Global Scale." *i-ItalyNY*, June-July, 10-12.

"Guido: An Italian-American Youth Style." i-Italy (special feature). http://www.i-italy.org/sections/specials/society/guido-italian-american-youth-style (accessed August 5, 2014).

Schneider, Jane, and Peter Schneider. 2014. "Reflecting on the Calandra Institute's 'MAFIAs: Realities and Representations of Organized Crime' Conference." *Il Bollettino* (newsletter) 7(1): 4.

Sciorra, Joseph. 2004. Review of *Heaven Touches Brooklyn in July*. *Journal of American Folklore* 117 (465): 459-462.

__________. 2014. "Why MAFIAs? Studying What Many Have Chosen to Ignore." i-Italy, April 14. http://www.i-italy.org/node/37822 (accessed August 5, 2014).

The Place of Italian American Studies in Italian Studies or What the Heck Does this Have to Do with Anything?

Graziella Parati
Dartmouth College

It is always fundamental for a scholar to establish her position vis-à-vis the academic work she is focusing on. Finding the scholar in the text is at times a rather self-indulgent operation, but, in this case quite an important one. At a recent meeting in which the Italian American Studies Network was created in Bellagio, Italy, the fact that only one Ivy League College teaches Italian American Culture came to light as quite astonishing news. In our ever-developing interests in hybridizations, global migrations, and accented writings, Italian American texts still play a secondary role in often very innovative English, American, and Italian culture departments.

Dartmouth College is that one Ivy League College where Italian American culture is regularly taught in a comparative literature department, cross-listed as a course in translation that counts toward the major and minor in Italian, and also as course for the minor in international studies. I teach that course that, during the spring quarter 2014, had thirty-eight students enrolled, a rather high number for a comparative literature, or an Italian class. Only three students were of Italian descent, five were Asian Americans, and two African American. A few were Latinos and Latinas, and the rest had Irish, German, English background. Some had been attracted by the title of the course "From Dagos to Sopranos," others were there because they knew about Italian American food, Guidos and Guidettes, mafia movies, or needed a course to graduate and thought that this course would be fun. They did not expect to learn much about American history, the construction of whiteness and race in general, and about radical movements they had never heard mentioned.

Some students took the class because they wanted to know more about Italy as they were bound to the peninsula for their study abroad program in art history. They expected to hear about the *bellezze* of Italy and acquire knowledge that would prepare them for being a tourist in the *Bel Paese*. They were betrayed in their expectations because this was a class devoted

From: *Transcending Borders, Bridging Gaps* (Calandra Institute, 2015)

to what tourists in Italy often ignore or, if they are interested, they are disappointed by the lack of knowledge of Italian migrations that they find in Italy. It has often happened that when Dartmouth alumni are on trips with a Dartmouth scholar, they want to find their roots hoping to discover their noble and famous ancestors. They attended Dartmouth and they expect to have forefathers that would match the prestige of their alma mater.

Narratives of poverty, of journeys made on ships and in third class, and of lives in New York City tenements were often the life stories of their ancestors. Some of my students at Dartmouth are children of a much more recent Italian migration than that which took place after WWI and are only second generation Italian Americans. For them the family memories turn for them into post-memories that are often quite distorted as well.

Therefore a course on Italian American culture often becomes a course on cultures and on interpretative approaches to multiple constructions of identity that encompass two continents and, above all, the many interpretations of Italy in the American cultural imagination. The seven majors in Italian that I had in my Spring class complained that we were not learning "enough" about Italy and that the history of dislocated Italianness was not really a course on Italy. However, a few weeks into the class, they realized that Italian America culture is as much a part of Italian history as it is a significant component of US history. The many interpretations of Italianness and of Italian Americanness create a tale of two cultures closely connected when viewed from the perspective of 20th and 21st century global diasporas.

For a long time silenced in Italian and U.S. academic curricula, Italian American Studies has emerged in the last thirty years as a useful field in the exploration of interstitial cultures. It has acquired status as a valid field of inquiry in the United States, but often remains "homeless" in academic terms. Some English and American studies departments house courses on the subject. We, at Dartmouth, teach Italian American culture in a comparative literature program in which cultural hybridity is a focus. I teach that course, but, although I have a joint title in comparative literature, I have a "home" in a traditional French and Italian department that, fortunately, accepts the cross-listing with comparative literature.

As we have moved away from only teaching the canon in Italian culture in the U.S., it is highly appropriate that Italian Departments begin to teach Italian American culture. Such a choice permits the repair of a mutilation in our curricula. It is vital that we expand what we mean by "Italian" or "Italianness" at a time in history when Italy must be recognized as a multicultural country. Contemporary Italian history connects uncannily with an Italian American past that allows contemporary experience of migrants to Italy to reflect the past experiences of Italian Americans. Paying attention these uncanny similarities can fruitfully allow the possibility of imagining the future of contemporary Italian culture in Italy and embrace the inevitable processes of hybridization taking place on the peninsula.

What is at stake is the relevance and the translation into practice of our studies on Italian culture in all its forms. Making room for Italian American courses in English/America, Italian, and comparative literature cultures allows us, the scholars, to be develop appropriate research at a time when Italy is going through a new process of nation building. The influx of migrants in Italy over the last 25 years has created the need to rethink the nation and the communities, with which Italians identify, through an inclusive process in which Italian American studies has much to contribute. There is no Italian studies right now that can afford to exclude Italian American studies. I would also add that there should no American studies without the inclusion of the multiplicity of hyphenated cultures that constitute American cultures. This is probably more easily acceptable, almost taken from granted, in American academic institutions. Unfortunately, that is not the case in Italian universities.

In their ground-breaking volume *Real Italians, New Immigrants: Interpreting Postwar Italian Migration to the United States* (University of Illinois Press, forthcoming), Laura E. Ruberto and Joseph Sciorra discuss migrations after WWII from Italy to the United States. Their innovative approach that emphasizes rarely studied waves of migration allows them to talk about the phenomenon of Italy's brain drain. I would count myself among that number of Italians who left their country of birth after completing a *laurea* (the old fashioned university program of 4 years plus a volume size thesis in the late 1980s). Although I studied American literature, I was completely ignorant about Italian American culture. It was only after arriving in the U.S. that my education began on this topic.

The brain drain from Italy seems to be accelerating in recent years. On May 29, 2014, the national newspaper *La stampa* has reported that 90,000 Italians migrated from Italy in 2011. Only 60,000 left in 2012, but that number rose to 75,000 in 2013, and it is projected that 100,000 Italian will migrate in 2014 (these are conservative estimates because only people officially registered as migrants can be counted). The number of Italians leaving the peninsula in 2014 will be higher than the number of migrants moving to Italy. This is a phenomenon that both Spain and Greece have already experienced. Half of the Italian e-migrants stay in Europe and some move to Germany, France and England, but others migrate to non-traditional countries of emigrations such as Rumania, Russia, and Hungary. Australia and the United States are some of the preferred destination countries outside of Europe, but China and Russia are gradually becoming other popular choices. The article also stresses that many of the people who migrated in recent years have a college degree[1] confirming the data supplied by the Italian institute for national statistics or ISTAT.[2] Whether in England, Germany, Australia or the United States, it is fundamental to be able to arrive in a new country with relevant knowledge about Italian history of migrations that are still drowned in silence in Italy's academic environment. Of course there are commendable exceptions. Some university professors have created courses in Italian universities that attempt to remedy to the traditional silence about the Italian diaspora and they must be recognized: Patrizia Ardizzone at the University of Naples, Leonardo Buonomo at the University of Trieste, Marina Camboni at the Univesrity of Macerata, Ottorino Cappelli and Donatella Izzo at the Università degli Studi of Naples "L'Orientale," Margherita Ganieri at the University of Calabria, Diego Lazzarich at the University of Naples II, Giorgio Mariani at the University "La Sapienza" in Rome, and, I would also like to include, Maddalena Tirabassi, director of the Centro Altreitalie, Globus and Locus in Turin, a city where the university offers a Master's degree in Italian American culture. All of them are founding members of the Italian American Studies Network.

In conclusion, there is only the hope that teaching Italian American and other migration cultures will allow recent migrants to build on the groundbreaking role that Italian Americans have played in the United States as innovators in politics, the arts, the sciences, and in creating practices in everyday life that are very visible in U.S. culture.

---

[1] http://fugadeitalenti.files.wordpress.com/2013/02/s24-indagine-altreitalie.pdf

[2] http://www.lastampa.it/2014/05/29/italia/cronache/di-nuovo-emigranti-pi-italiani-in-fuga-che-stranieri-in-arrivo-5iy5XYiDRFl5oW0npAG68J/pagina.html.
See also: http://fugadeitalenti.files.wordpress.com/2013/02/s24-indagine-altreitalie.pdf.

Italian/American Components within Italian Studies

Margherita Ganeri
University of Calabria

The main purpose of this historic conference in Bellagio, the first ever of its type, is to elaborate new strategies for the promotion of Italian/American Studies as a recognized academic field in the Italian university system. The timing seems to be ideal, as I shall try to demonstrate here. As a premise to our goal, it is necessary, of course, to reflect on the current state of the debate on Italian/American studies in Italy. But it is even more necessary, in my point of view, to clarify those academic disciplines that, with regard to the US, are very differently conceived in Italy.

The expression itself, "Italian Studies," is not completely translatable into Italian, as we do not have a general discipline covering all the different areas it refers to in the American university system. The so-called *Italianistica* is still intended to be strictly the study of Italian literature. In some dictionaries it includes also the language. I find most accurate the definition offered by the *Enciclopedia Treccani*, which says: "il complesso delle discipline settoriali in cui si articola lo studio specialistico della letteratura italiana"[1] (the complex of sectorial disciplines related to the specialistic study of Italian literature). In fact, *Italianistica* excludes not only the various academic disciplines devoted to researching Italian language (such as *Linguistica italiana* and *Storia della lingua italiana*), but also all the others dedicated to any aspect of Italian culture, from history to anthropology, from art to music, from cinema to TV and media. It includes only Italian literature, together with both philology and criticism.

Not only do we maintain a strong differentiation among humanistic areas, as literature, cinema, visual arts, music and so on, but we have different disciplines inside each of these fields. Each employed professor or researcher working in any Italian university was hired through a series of competitions focused on specific areas of expertise. The teaching of Italian Literature, which excludes the teaching of the language, is divided in two

---

[1] See Treccani on line: http://www.treccani.it/enciclopedia/italianistica/

From: *Transcending Borders, Bridging Gaps* (Calandra Institute, 2015)

different so-called "scientific-disciplinary sectors": *Letteratura italiana* and *Letteratura italiana contemporanea*.[2] The first one is supposed to cover, as the name says, the history of Italian literature from the beginning to the present, but in reality it covers the centuries before the nineteen hundreds. The second one, in contrast with its name, covers a little less than the last two centuries up to the present: for some, starting from the early Romantic period, for others, from the years of the Risorgimento, for the majority from the Unification of Italy (1861). I will get back to this later.

These areas are conceived, in Italy, as distinct research specialties, but also as different teaching disciplines. For example, as a professor of contemporary Italian literature, I teach only courses related to the nineteenth and twentieth centuries, with references to the present. I do not teach language courses, nor courses on Dante, Boccaccio, Machiavelli, or Ariosto. And I do research almost exclusively in my field of specialty, as I am expected (and periodically inspected) to do. The recent institution of a national evaluating board to confer the so-called *Abilitazione Scientifica Nazionale* (National Scientific Habilitation) for university professors by the Minister of Education,[3] even though registering some unifications of smaller scientific sectors in larger so-called macro-sectors, still reflects this specialized context. In order to be promoted, candidates submit for evaluation only their publications that would fit into each sector, and therefore generally choose their research subjects among the suitable ones for one of them.

There are, of course, various and complex historical reasons that explain this specific situation of Italian studies in Italy. It is not my aim here to discuss them. The only one I would like to address is one of the less significant, and is that so-called cultural studies, to quote the definition credited to Richard Hoggart, and later mostly associated with Stuart Hall, were never influential in Italy. Theorists like Stephen Greenblatt, Edward Said, Gayatri Chakravorty Spivak, just to mention only a few leading names among the most internationally recognized, offered, from different perspectives, a theoretical account for a series of social and anthropological

---

[2] Some smaller sectors, as Medieval Italian Literature, Theory of Literature and Criticism, even though still autonomously existing in same universities, have been recently unified with the "Letteratura Italiana" macro-sector.

[3] "Abilitazione scientifica nazionale" (ASN) official Web site is: http://abilitazione.miur.it/public/index.php.

phenomena that were developing within the contemporary period, phenomena that create the need for reflection on the shape of the postcolonial Mac World. And, of course, feminist criticism, and later gender studies, also played a very important role in this debate, as they did in the more vast and perhaps more controversial international discussion of the last part of the twentieth century, the debate on the canon as a male, white, and western-oriented hegemony. It is thus not surprising that the Italian academic mainstream, and especially the most prominent names in *Italianistica*, were never influenced by feminist criticism or by gender studies, just as they were snobbishly refusing to reflect on the new issues brought up by the best advocates of Cultural Studies. There has always been a certain delay in Italy in the matter of innovation. The Italian intellectual mainstream has always been very conservative.

Apart for some essential references, I will not address here the scholarly state of Italian Americana in Italy.[4] The aim of my intervention is to defend the idea that it can be introduced into the Italian university system not only trough the sector of the American studies, but also, and in my point of view very fruitfully, through that of contemporary Italian literature.

The debate on Migration literature developed into a regular discussion in Italy only in the 1990s. The diffusion of Italian/American Studies, viewed—within *Italianistica*—as a specific field of this debate, is even later. In the Preface to the first edition of the anthology *From the Margin, Writings in Italian Americana*,[5] the editors Tamburri, Giordano and Gardaphé describe the situation of these studies in the United States, during the 1980s, as still very controversial and poor in size. In Italy at that time it was almost totally non-existent.

Today, the discussion is not on the table in Italy, as it is in North America, even though it will surely grow, since it is gaining more and

---

[4] I addressed this in the first chapter of my book on Helen Barolini: M. Ganeri, *L'America italiana. Epos e storytelling in Helen Barolini* (Arezzo: Zona, 2010), now in English translation with Mimesis International; and in the article: M. Ganeri, "The Broadening of the Concept of «Migration Literature» in Contemporary Italy," *Forum Italicum*, vol. 44, n. 2, 2010, pp. 437-451.

[5] Tamburri Anthony Julian, Paolo A. Giordano, and Fred L. Gardaphé, eds., *From the Margin. Writings in Italian Americana*, revised edition (West Lafayette, IN: Purdue University Press, 2000 [1991]).

more attention. But it is still marginal in contemporary Italian hegemonic academia, and particularly in the field of *Italianistica*.

Why did the discussions about migrant literature only begin to spread throughout Italy in the late 1990s? Of course the broad background of this interest is the debate on postmodernism. The more specific background is the debate on multiculturalism and multi-ethnicity, which was first explored in the United States. But the new interest arose also as a consequence of the explosion of problems related to the massive numbers of immigrants who arrived in the country in the last two to three decades. The former phenomena regarding Italians migrating abroad were neglected for a very long time. The latter cannot be ignored, because it is happening inside the country. Literary works written in Italian by foreigners living in Italy have been increasingly challenging, and inevitably threatening the self-perception of a pure national literary tradition.

Like it or not, Italy is becoming a multiethnic environment. Schools and universities are increasingly attended by foreign and foreign-origin students. There is already a second generation of college students, and one third of school-age children born in Italy. Italian society is going trough a process of deep transformation, due to the consistent presence of migrants. Cultural and linguistic integration has already become a necessary requirement in the educational system. And just as migration is a central issue in the political agenda, migration literature is becoming a crucial question to be addressed by scholars and teachers. This is why the Bellagio conference comes at a very good time.

Apart from scholarly production and from editorial visibility, the best way to promote the spread of Italian/American literary studies is through the institution of teaching programs and curricula in universities and, potentially, in high schools. I am convinced that the timing is ideal for this too. Of course, the proper, natural space for it is the discipline of American Language and Literature. But I think another larger space could be found in Contemporary Italian Literature.

In which scientific sector of the Italian academia are we supposed to study migrant writers such as Erminia dell'Oro, Gabriella Ghermandi, Amara Lakhous, or Igiaba Scego, just to name a few among my favorites ones? Of course they will be included in contemporary Italian literature, as they are novelists who write in Italian. There are, of course, not yet built into the hegemonic canon, but at least same of them will be recognized, for sure, in the future.

Why couldn't we include Italian/American writers? The obvious general answer is because they write in English. But this is not always true, as we know very well, here. Especially the first volume of the impressive anthology edited by Francesco Durante, covering almost a century up to 1880, contains mostly texts in Italian,[6] and through the end of the 1930s it is more common, as Durante writes in the preface, to find writers who still use their original language. It is less common later, but a few are bilingual still today. This means that technically the best of them could be included in the Italian canon. But also the ones who write only in English can be included, if not in the canon, at least in school anthologies and histories, and in course syllabi on modern and contemporary Italian literature, using translations or, when possible, offering a percentage of classes in English, which are anyway becoming compulsory in the Italian universities, due to the new European Union rules regarding higher education. I tend to agree with the larger school of thought that believes it is mostly the language that defines the identity of a literary repertoire, even though I am aware of the fact that this idea raises several problems. But we have to constantly broaden our vision when studying and teaching our national literature. Translations must be welcome, if they allow us to achieve this goal.

Contemporary Italian literature, as I mentioned before, is supposed to start in the second part of the nineteenth century, with Italy's national Unification. But until now its borders have not included migrant writers, not even African writers from the ex-colonies, and had excluded the massive records of the so-called Great Migration, which depended mostly on post-unification national politics. These are crucial removals to finally recuperate. Writers such as Verga, Maria Messina, Pirandello, and, later, Sciascia, among others, have written occasionally on the poorest masses of people who were forced to leave Sicily for America. Why was their testi-

---

[6] *Italoamericana. Storia e letteratura degli Italiani negli Stati Uniti*, edited by Francesco Durante, two volumes (I [1776-1880], Mondadori, 2001; II [1880-1943], Mondadori, 2005). The second volume has been recently translated in English: *Italoamericana. The Literature of the Great Migration, 1880-1943*, edited by Francesco Durante; General Editor of the American Edition: Robert Viscusi; Translations Editor: Anthony Julian Tamburri; Bibliographic Editor: James J. Periconi (New York: Fordham University Press, 2014).

mony, in this respect, so much ignored by scholars? Lower-class poverty and unemployment, dismissal and indifference on the part of the Italian government, the so-called Southern Question, the African military wars of colonial conquest: these are all fundamental elements of the historical context, necessary to understand the literature of this age. And this goes without mentioning the debate on world literature, which works again the concept itself of a national canon, as Remo Ceserani, among others, has recently pointed out.[7]

I am sure everybody believes today that many writings by Italian Americans are related to Italy. Very often they have a lot to do with Italy and it is a shame that Italy has not given, until recently, much consideration to them, as many have denounced. It is obvious, due to the massive numbers emigrating from Italy to North and South America, Australia, and Northern Europe since the 1860s, that in novels, short stories, dramas, plays, poetries, as well as in films, and in other art products by the emigrants and by their descendants, Italy and Italian culture have a relevant role. The relevance itself of the phenomenon justifies a consideration of this artistic repertoire as part of Italian cultural history, regardless of the languages used. If they are part of the history, they should be also part of the history of literature. In previous published works I had written the opposite on this issue, but with time and reflection I have changed idea.[8]

How could *Italianistica*, at least that of the modern and contemporary sector, remain attached to its old-fashion traditional closeness? It cannot, unless it decides to die. It has been recognized for a long time that the European framework is necessary to understand every single Italian contemporary writer. You cannot read Verga without Zola, De Roberto without Flaubert, D'Annunzio without Huysmans, Svevo without Freud, Tomasi of Lampedusa without Proust, and so on. Today comparative, multilingual, intersected perspectives are more necessary than in the past. And with Italian Americana the intersection is based on history, and it is therefore the strongest one you can possibly have.

I was happily surprised by the intervention of Donatella Izzo, included in this publication, as it completely confirmed my idea that the best way to introduce Italian/American Studies in Italy would be through the Italian

[7] See in particular Giuliana Benvenuti and Remo Ceserani, *La letteratura nell'età globale* (Bologna: Il Mulino, 2012).

[8] I am referring to publications listed in footnote n. 4.

Studies, and not as much as through the field of American Studies. First of all, Italian Studies is obviously a much larger sector in the national university system: American Studies is not offered in all the universities, while Italian literature is one of the basic courses everywhere for all the Humanities degrees. But the main reason is another. I agree with Donatella about the fact that Italian students who choose to pursue curricula in American Studies are interested in learning what in their point of view is really American. Italian/American Studies is still not adequately recognized as part of the American canon, and at the same time it sounds too Italian for these students. On the contrary, especially graduate students who specialize in Italian literature, and for instance those who concentrate on the modern period, can develop strong interest and motivation toward Italian/American Studies. I have had several occasions to verify this in class, even though I do not have an official survey as the very interesting one Donatella has proposed here. My experience pushes me to believe that students of Contemporary Italian Literature are and will be more interested than others, because they are generally very much interested in the new migrant literature that spread throughout Italy in the 1990s as a consequence of the massive numbers of immigrants who arrived in the last two to three decades.

In my courses in these past few years I have regularly included migrant contemporary writers who write in Italian, novels on the Great Migration, such as *Vita* by Melania Mazzucco, and some Italian/American writers, especially Helen Barolini. Students were always very interested, and I have tutored several theses on these topics, unlike Donatella. When Anthony Tamburri and Fred Gardaphé came to the University of Calabria in November 2013 to teach two intensive weeks of seminars for our graduate students, even though the course in which they were lecturing was entitled "Contemporary Italian Literature," which is my officially assigned course, their classes were very successful among the almost one hundred students attending.

As Izzo pointed out about the Orientale in Naples, the University of Calabria is also attended mostly by students coming from the region and from its surroundings. Practically every student has some history of migration in their families, and has relatives abroad. Nonetheless, in my opinion their interest does not depend as much on their personal memories as on their perception of a current difficult situation, very similar to that which forced the old emigrants to leave. Migrants arriving daily and dramatically often dying on the sea constitute an everyday scenario on the Calabrian costs, as on the Sicilian. In Crotone there is the larger reception centre for them in Europe, the principal among the many Lager-type concentration camps called "centri di prima accoglienza." Being from the region with the highest rate of unemployment, Calabrian graduates know that they will have to emigrate at the end of their studies, or they will be stuck with a very poor future, and especially the ones who graduate in literature and in humanities. Italian/American writers as Pietro Di Donato, Mario Puzo, John Fante, and Don DeLillo narrate different aspects of contemporary social conflicts and alienation. This is why, in my point of view, the students I have taught appreciate them.

Gardaphé's and Tamburri's seminars were so successful that, together with Marta Petrusewicz, Professor of Modern History, who moved from CUNY to UniCal, I decided to propose to the Director of our Department of Humanistic Studies, Professor Raffaele Perrelli, the institution of a full one-semester course on Italian/American Culture and Literature. The request was approved, and the course was established for the graduate degree of "*Laurea magistrale*" (two-year level, similar to the U.S. Master of Arts) in Modern Languages and Literatures. With the title in Italian ("Cultura e Letteratura italiana americana," shortened in CLIA), but taught in English, it has started in the first semester of the academic year 2014-2015, and it is a compulsory course for the students who have to gain credits for contemporary Italian literature, approximately fifty.

As far as we know, this is the first official full course on Italian/American literature in Italy. Due to the intense cooperation with Tamburri and Gardaphé, who are coming regularly to teach at UniCal, we have established a long-term agreement with Calandra Institute and Queen's college of the City University of New York. Favored by the highest administrative body of our institution, particularly from our *Rettore*, Professor Gino Mirocle Crisci, and from our *Prorettore*, Professor Guerino D'Ignazio, and supported by two departments (humanistic studies and political and social sciences), our road map for the future includes teaching and researching activities on migrations, on Italian cultures abroad, and on Italian Americana. The institution of the above mentioned course is the first achievement. In June 2015 we hope to be able to guest the first international Summer School on Italian Diasporas, open worldwide to doctoral students who would want to participate. I am very grateful to Tamburri and Gardaphé for their generous efforts on these projects, and I would like to thank also Peter Carravetta, who was born in Calabria, near our university's town, and Paul Giordano, who both came to teach in CLIA 2014, together with the independent scholar Sam Patti, attached to the University of Pittsburgh (Pennsylvania).

With these thrilling and stimulating programs, and with the cooperation of colleagues from different fields and universities, we wish to establish at the University of Calabria a recognized interdisciplinary centre of research on Italian migrations in and out. We think Calabria offers an ideal geographical and cultural environment to interrogate these phenomena.

Underdevelopment, unemployment, economical crisis, political corruption and the enormous power of the local, very strong criminal organization, the *'ndrangheta*, render particularly acute and visible, in the southern part of the Italian peninsula, the multiple problems and contradictions that afflict present Italy. Calabria today is no longer an archaic land where nothing happens, but it is a vibrant iper-modern periphery where economic and social conflicts develop with extreme and explosive impact. It is precisely for its troubled marginality that the poorest Italian region might offer the possibility of a better viewing of the global. As in psychoanalytic therapy, what happens in the margins is often more meaningful and brings insight toward the centre. This is why, in its degraded scenario, Calabria could qualify itself as a privileged observatory of the ultimate consequences of the economies of the Mac World, and, of course, as one of the best places, in Italy, from where to dominate the scene of present migrations in the shade of the previous historical ones.

We hope Calabria could also become an attractive area to spend short periods of study, especially for Italian/American scholars and students. Many of them have Calabrian origins, and generally the cultural heritage of the region is felt very strongly by the people who left it, as several writers recall it, from Helen Barolini to Mark Rotella to the recent *My two Italies* by Joseph Luzzi, just to mention some examples. Due to its large number of emigrants in time and space, we may jokingly state that Calabria is probably more abroad than at the toe of the boot. Nonetheless, due to its economical and cultural depression, it is rarely visited for touristic purposes, and therefore is very little known, not even by descendants of Calabrians.

Returning to the topic of contemporary *Italianistica*, introducing migrant literatures will work against the conservative attitude of the Italian academic establishment. We should work to change it, it is time for a radical change. There is a confined but very qualified scholarly production in Italy dedicated to Italian Americana. Scholars such as Francesco Durante, Martino Marazzi, Sebastiano Martelli, among others, have written excellent books and articles. Martelli is Professor of *Letteratura italiana* at the University of Salerno. The other two were recently awarded the "Abilitazione scientifica nazionale" in the same sector, based on the recognition of quality, but also of pertinence, of their publications within it. Their academic discipline is still neglecting diaspora writers, but these are good signs, as many others all around, about a substantial change in this regard in the near future.

The disciplinary statute of Italian Literature, especially the modern and contemporary sector, has to be enlarged. We have to fight for a shared consideration of Italian/American Studies as a field so closely related to it in order to have the potentiality to become an effective component, at least from Italy's unification on.

Quoting the title of one of Gardaphé's book, *Italian signs, American Streets*, in contemporary Italy it is now time for the reversed search, as we could productively look for American signs on Italian streets. This will still be, as Gardaphé states, "a process that, for its advocate, necessarily involves a self-politicization that requires placing a personal item onto a public agenda."[9] To be candid, I do not think Italian scholars and students could be interested in searching for the supposed existence of an essential *italianità*, permeated by "ethnic tension," as Gardaphé maintains, but we can contribute to the renovation of the field by recognizing Italian/ American Studies as legitimate components within *Italianistica*, conceived in a broader national sense. Cultural Studies can play a role in transforming our sense of literary national tradition from local to global. And, in this respect I am sure we could find some space to exercise that personal criticism Gardaphé and others indicate as preferable. After all, contemporary Italians are in many ways Americanized, mostly due to the influence of

---

[9] Fred L. Gardaphé, *Italian Signs, American Streets. The Evolution of Italian American Narrative* (Durham: Duke University Press, 1996). Italian translation: *Segni italiani, strade americane: l'evoluzione della letteratura italiana Americana* (Florence: Cesati, 2012). Quotations from pages 1-4 of the English edition.

cinema and TV. Therefore we could even think of ourselves as specific new types of Italian Americans. In all seriousness, it is important to pursue new perspectives based on a renovated sense of intertwinement among the two shores and elsewhere there may be communities of Italian origins.

In his most recent book, Anthony Tamburri strongly defends the point of the continued existence of Italian/American literature and of the fact that it has renewed itself with new powerful paradigms, resulting in an "*epistemological collision.*"[10] He is sure the field has acquired today new potentials, that is to say:

> [T]he potential to cast aside the old lens of the monolith and reconsider Italian/American literature through a more prismatic lens that allow us to see the different nooks and crannies of out ethnicity as it has changed over the decades and across generations from a dualistic discourse to a multifaceted conglomeration of cultural processes transgressing Italian, American (read, here, also Canada and United States, as one indeed should), and Italian/American cultural borders. (157)

This quote from the ending paragraph of the book — almost identical to a previous statement ten pages earlier (146), and probably to reinforce the author's beliefs and hopes of continuous innovation — presents us with a vision of the Italian/American critical battlefield as an open space, potentially without borders.

I am sure this potentiality of transgressing borders, bridging gaps, and bringing enlargement and enrichment could be very well understood and fight for by Italian scholars and students of contemporary Italian literature, especially from those coming from the margins of the south of Italy.

---

[10] Anthony Julian Tamburri, *Re-reading Italian Americana: Specificities and Generalities on Literature and Criticism* (Madison, NJ: Fairleigh Dickinson University Press, 2014) 155.

Falling Through the Cracks
Italian America, Literary Studies, and the Academy

Mary Jo Bona
Stony Brook University

In a 2008 episode of *Jeopardy* (a quiz competition game show in the U.S.), the $800 clue under the category "20th Century Novels" featured this declaration: "In 1955 he got an offer he couldn't refuse: the publication of his first novel, 'The Dark Arena.'" Neither knowledge of the author's *oeuvre* nor the focus of his postwar novel were needed to answer correctly, in the required form of a question, "Who is Mario Puzo?" The most famous—or infamous—idiom in Italian American parlance goes hands-down to Mario Puzo, whose Don Corleone utters this statement, and, like Nora's slamming door, the sound reverberated round the world, especially through its cinematic incarnation in Francis Ford Coppola's film. While those of us working to develop the field of Italian American Studies, and, in particular, its literature, Puzo's *The Godfather* has always presented both a challenge and a burden.

The alignment of a particular ethnicity, in this case, Italian, with criminality, in American history is neither new nor exciting, but has troubled Italian Americans since at least the 1880s, when stiletto-wielding Black Handers were featured on the pages of *The New York Harold*. With the 1969 publication of *The Godfather*, Puzo brilliantly managed to resurrect and romanticize the criminal figure by creating a god in Don Corleone, whose distancing measures (from the sordid world of narcotics, for example) reflect Puzo's will to canon within a middle-brow book of popular fiction. Such brilliance poses a challenge for scholars who must approach the novel on several fronts, accepting the fact that "*The Godfather* has done more to create a national consciousness of the Italian American experience than any work of fiction or nonfiction published before or since" (Gardaphé 89). Puzo's literary forbears, Bernadino Ciambelli, Garibaldi Lapolla, Guido D'Agostino, Pietro di Donato, and John Fante (all of whom he read voraciously) prepared him to extend the critique of American capitalism through the filter of Sicilian American family justice, paving the way

From: *Transcending Borders, Bridging Gaps* (Calandra Institute, 2015)

in the second half of the twentieth century for the creation of Don DeLillo's filmmaker, Frank Volterra, of *The Names*, whose comment that "Italians have made the family an extremist group" (202), reverberates around the cottage industry produced by *The Godfather*. How indebted is Italian American literature to *The Godfather*? Tremendously so. *Purtroppo*? I think not.

The obligation for scholars of Italian America in traditional disciplines such as English, Italian, and comparative literature, is to find ways to incorporate works on syllabi without performing minoritizing gestures like including such works under the rubric of "recommended," without ever teaching them. Or, worse, to my way of thinking, including a cinematic interlude in a literature course, but failing to introduce students to the literary contributions of Italian Americans. For one of the central ways Italian American *literary* works have been revitalized is through the intertwining activities of book reprinting and classroom teaching. Certainly the publishing contributions of Guernica Editions and Bordighera Press have gone far in making and keeping visible the contributions of Italian Canadian and American writers. When all is said and done, the classroom and the syllabus insure the book maintains visibility and, whether or not it is taught to students as non-canonical, it is received, as Jeffrey Insko explains, by students as canonical (346), echoing John Guillory's assertion that individual works "confront their receptors first as canonical, as cultural capital" (56). The very novels we have striven to get back into publication is an act of custodianship: we minimize the risk of further loss by the dual activities of safekeeping and claiming.

Yet this does not solve the problem of teaching Puzo's *The Godfather* in the university classroom, since popular fiction has been disparaged or at least found suspect among English professors since the professionalization of reading developed as an academic endeavor. As we recall, Harriet Beecher Stowe's magnificent *Uncle Tom's Cabin* was relegated to the historical shelves and faulted in the twentieth century for its sentimentalism (among other things). Puzo himself denigrated the very genre of popular fiction that gave him his greatest success and fame, admitting that he "wrote below his gifts in that novel." While it is not my purpose in this forum to argue for Puzo's canonization within the category of "Great Books," *The Godfather* remains an example of a *classic* novel, like Stowe's, in the popular fiction category, and, as such, the novel "perhaps more than any other kind of literature, has always blurred the distinction between popular and high art" (Torgovnick 114).

The erasure of literary Italian America, whether popular or elite, was neither entirely systemic nor systematic, but occurred in the 1930s along with the elimination of black, white female, and all working-class writers from the American literary canon. As Paul Lauter adumbrated, "the professionalization of the teaching of literature, the development of an aesthetic theory that privileged certain texts, and the historiographic organization of the body of literature into conventional 'periods' and 'themes' (27) creates intrinsic barriers to teaching lesser known writers. The hegemonic force of American literary anthologies, which decreased focus on a variety of writers in favor of promoting "major writers," all but guaranteed the exclusion of ethnically identified writers from syllabi. Along with primarily Anglo-Saxon male professors, who influenced the teaching of literature and reading choices, were editors themselves, who, in their untested acceptance of the inherent value of certain literary works, did not or refused to *recognize* "their own role in determining which are the truly great works" (Tompkins 188).

For all the publication successes of writers such as Fante, di Donato, and Jerre Mangione in the 1930s and 1940s, they did not reap the benefits of sustained secondary criticism or anthology inclusion (within the academy) until the latter half of the twentieth century. Nonetheless their narratives and the many others alongside them unflinchingly portray being colonized by a homeland that starved them and a new world that exploited them. Those of us devoted to the ongoing recovery work of Italian American writers recognize that we are chin-deep involved in determining how this literature will be valued and interpreted in the future. As a result, we must move outside the still limiting confines of traditional departments in order to introduce underrepresented texts, aware of the intersection between redefined modes of scholarship and pedagogy.

As a professor in the humanities at a state institution in New York, I am quite aware of the rough-hewn history of Italian American studies in the academy. That Stony Brook University can boast a minor in this discipline is no small feat; the demography of Long Island and a longstanding tradition in the community of honoring Italian heritage (however traditionally defined it may be) enabled such a disciplinary study to come to fruition within the academy. On eastern Long Island, where Stony Brook

of the material conditions that somehow enabled these women's survival through differing kinds of mobility.

No less fruitful would be to place two, generically different works by the same author side-by-side, thereby inflecting the experience of reading them together. Puzo's second novel, *The Fortunate Pilgrim*, allows readers to deconstruct the romance of the third, provoking a rereading of *The Godfather* that *resists* the tendency to be seduced by the world of *comparatico* represented by the enclosure of Sicilian Americans. Add to this example of provincialism a feminist reading and a woman might ask the same question that Judith Fetterley suggests she ask about that earlier misogynistic tale of America, "Rip Van Winkle": what is a woman to do? Like Irving's seductively amiable tale, Puzo's novel invites the female reader to be "co-opted into participation in an experience from which she is explicitly excluded; she is asked to identify with a selfhood that defines itself in opposition to her; she is required to identify against herself" (Fetterley, 9, xii). For in *The Godfather*, there is only one person with whom to identify—Don Corleone—and the identification is illusory and impossible for any reader, resisting or not. When juxtaposed to *The Fortunate Pilgrim*, however, *The Godfather* can be deconstructed and the very mythology of Sicilian justice critiqued by its central character, Lucia Santa, whose resiliency and strength emerge from an impregnable understanding of honor and loyalty disconnected from masculine notions of power.

Such comparative approaches to teaching in ethnic studies programs like Italian American Studies spurs a renewal in thinking across programs and in freshly emerging disciplinary fields. As a self-identified professor of Italian American studies and women's and gender studies, my move into a newly merged department at Stony Brook has enabled a more fluid approach to my teaching and scholarship. The Department of Cultural Analysis and Theory houses programs in women's and gender studies, comparative literature and Cultural Studies, and, along with my affiliated department of English, I am better able to focus in the expanded disciplinary fields within American literature, inclusive of multiethnic (read also, Italian American), women's literature and feminist theory; and theories of diaspora, ethnicity, and migration. Described as a dynamic trans-disciplinary space for the scholarly exchange of methods and concepts for analyzing complex social and cultural phenomena, my department accepts prima facie that scholarship has become much more interdisciplinary and literary scholars and texts have been relocated "to unfamiliar territory" (Elliott & Stokes, 1). For those of us who have been involved from the outset in program building in the fields of Women's and Gender Studies and Italian American Studies, we early endeavored to introduce new area studies, so the experience of broaching disciplinary limits and collaborating across disciplines has become standard operating procedure.

My disciplinary focus in producing scholarship in Italian American Studies, women's literature, and multiethnic American literature, has persuaded me and scholars from my generation to recognize the necessity of program building within the university in order to examine the relationships between textual analysis and extra-literary sources (e.g., oral testimony, political speeches, advertising, food, sermons, laws and legal tracts). Thus, in the late 1980s, while working in my scholarly life on literary Italian America, I was concurrently collaborating with colleagues from multiple disciplines at Gonzaga University to build the inaugural program in Women's and Gender Studies there. This kind of program building—interdisciplinary and collaborative—continues today, and, along with increasing recognition of what feminist critics like to call intersectionality (the study of race, gender, class, sexuality, e.g.), scholars enter into formal conversations not only about the history of women's civil rights but also about the making of American literature and its gradual but measured removal of women's voices.

These two disciplinary areas—American literature and Women's and Gender Studies—inform each other and enabled me to shift my thinking in a curricular manner toward Italian American studies, permitting the move to Stony Brook in 1999, where, with Fred Gardaphé, we built the minor in Italian American Studies. The syllabi we developed for the minor reflects the fundamentally interdisciplinary nature of this area study, traversing traditional disciplinary boundaries represented at U.S. universities in departments of History, Sociology, and English, and simultaneously engaging with evolving disciplines such as cinema/film/visual media studies, cultural studies, and Women's and Gender Studies.

The academic shifts in the 1970s and 1980s that brought conversations—often contentious—about canon reformation to the forefront, and in the 1990s, brought the "cultural wars" to a fever pitch, required us to work fast and proficiently to develop the late arriving field of Italian American Studies. Aware that academic canons exert hegemonic force in traditional departments, we worked to align our classes with general education requirements for idealistic and pragmatic purposes: to expose a larger swath of the Stony Brook student population to the field of Italian Americana and to assure that our courses would garner the numbers to keep them running. Donning several hats beyond what counts in academia as promotion worthy, those of us who have built programs recognize the necessity of promoting the discipline in various venues, importantly in our communities, bridging distances between town and gown. It seems to me that our Bellagio Forum, "Transcending Borders: Bridging Gaps: Italian Americans, Diasporic Studies and the University Curriculum," not only reflects work thus far completed, but also recognizes the necessity of moving beyond foundational paradigms in order to reinvigorate our presence within academia. Just as other fields have encouraged me as a literary critic to respond to the new critical idea of singular literary language with an approach that bridges text and context, so also has the field of Italian American Studies invited new historicist approaches that address social and political contexts that enrich literary analysis. As Jane Tompkins said, "*literary* judgments of value do not [solely] depend on literary considerations alone, since the notion of what is literary is defined by and nested within changing historical conditions" (195).

If the field of Italian American Studies falls through the cracks in academia, then it is up to us to get on our knees and start digging. Those of us in this forum appreciate the inseparable nexus of manuscript publishing, personal advocacy, word-of-mouth sponsorship, supportive publishers, scholarly critiques, conference panels, books, exhibits, and, not the least—syllabi inclusion. Lest we despair, let us remember that during the terrible Depression of the 1930s, the literary landscape shifted, illuminating the works immigrant and minority writers, including Italian Americans. Consider the careers of John Fante, Pietro di Donato, Jerre Mangione, Mari Tomasi, Marion Benasutti, and certainly, Frances Winwar. The scholars represented in our Bellagio forum have been at the vanguard of this disciplinary area; it is up to us to increase visibility, continue our publication efforts, and pass the baton to the next generation of scholars. And, should fortuitous events embrace us, I imagine here a future episode of *Jeopardy*, in which, under the category of "20th-Century Novels," the $2,000 clue reads as follows: "In her only published novel of Italian American Chicago, this author wrote the line, "'When you fight to come home, you beautiful.'"

WORKS CITED

Bona, Mary Jo. *By the Breath of Their Mouths: Narratives of Resistance in Italian America*. Albany, NY: State University of New York Press, 2010.

_______. "Puzo and the Power of Fictional Mythography." *Voices in Italian Americana* 19.2 (Fall 2008): 28-42.

DeLillo, Don. *The Names*. New York: Vintage, 1992.

Elliott, Michael A. and Claudia Stokes, eds. Introduction. *American Literary Studies: A Methodological Reader*. New York and London: New York University Press, 2003. 1-15.

Fetterley, Judith. *The Resisting Reader: A Feminist Approach to American Fiction*. Bloomington: Indiana University Press, 1978.

Gardaphé, Fred L. *Italian Signs, American Streets: The Evolution of Italian American Narrative*. Durham: Duke University Press, 1996.

Guillory, John. *Cultural Capital: The Problem of Literary Canon Formation*. Chicago: University of Chicago Press, 1993.

Insko, Jeffrey. "Generational Canons." *Pedagogy: Critical Approaches to Teaching Literature, Language, Composition, and Culture*. 3.3 (2003): 341-358.

Lauter, Paul. *Canons and Contexts*. New York: Oxford University Press, 1991.

Messenger, Chris. *The Godfather and American Culture: How the Corleones Became "Our Gang."* Albany: State University of New York Press, 2002.

Morrison, Toni. "Unspeakable Things Unspoken: The Afro-American Presence in American Literature." *Modern Critical Views: Toni Morrison*. Ed. Harold Bloom. New York: Chelsea, 1990. 201-230.

Palumbo-Liu, David, ed. Introduction. *The Ethnic Canon: Histories, Institutions and Interventions*. Minneapolis: University of Minnesota Press, 1995. 1-27.

Sanders, Mark A. "Brief Reflections on the Discourse of Transnationalism and African American Studies." Ethnic Studies in the Age of Transnationalism. *PMLA* 122.3 (May 2007): 812-814.

Tompkins, Jane. *Sensational Designs: The Cultural Work of American Fiction, 1790-1860*. New York: Oxford University Press, 1985.

Torgovnick, Marianna, De Marco. *Crossing Ocean Parkway*. Chicago: University of Chicago Press, 1994.

VIA: Voices in Italian Americana: a literary and cultural review. Special Issue: Reconsidering Mario Puzo. Eds. Chris Messenger, Michele Fazio and JoAnne Ruvoli. 19.2. 2008.

BETWEEN AMERICA'S ITALY AND ITALY'S AMERICA

Leonardo Buonomo
UNIVERSITY OF TRIESTE

In my very early years at the University of Trieste I taught, as one did, whatever was needed, or what no one else wanted to teach, in the English curriculum, which could range from the *Mystery Plays* to John Bunyan to Samuel Richardson's *Pamela*. However, as a gracious concession to my background in American literature, I was allowed to use two hours a week to read with a select, highly motivated group of students the works of Hawthorne, Melville, Thoreau, and other canonical authors from across the Atlantic. In those years, when I put my "American literature" hat on, I worked alongside William Boelhower, author of the (by now) classic *Immigrant Autobiography in the United States*, and it was he who gave me the chance to devise and conduct for the first time a seminar on a topic of *my own* choice. And so it was that I put together a reading list which included some of the writers I would continue to work on for many years to come—Luigi Palma di Cesnola, Sister Blandina Segale, Emanuel Carnevali, John Fante, Jerre Mangione, and even a living one I had met in the flesh, Mary Bucci Bush—and called it "Italian Americana: Narratives in Search of Identity." Only the students who attended that seminar would be entitled to say if it was a success or not, but I do take pride in the fact that, with its exclusive focus on Italian American writing, it was the first of its kind at the University of Trieste.

I had discovered some of these writers, and indeed the field of Italian American studies itself, primarily through Boelhower and two landmark anthologies: *The Dream Book*, edited by Helen Barolini, and *From the Margin*, edited by Fred Gardaphé, Paolo Giordano, and Anthony Tamburri. But what had also steered me in that direction, and had induced me to think of Italian American writing in the larger context of American studies, was the work I had been doing on nineteenth-century American writers in Italy. Having examined the point of view of Americans who had come over here, it seemed only natural to develop an interest in those Italians who had taken, for a number of reasons, the opposite trajectory, *and*

From: *Transcending Borders, Bridging Gaps* (Calandra Institute, 2015)

in their descendants. I was reminded of how closely these two areas of interest were inter-related every time I searched for sources relating to American writing about Italy in online library catalogues. Invariably, my rather unsophisticated combination of the words "America," (or "United States"), "Italy," and "writing/writers" produced a list of entries which included works about both the "American Italian" *and* the Italian American experience. Indeed it was while doing this type of electronic fishing at the library of the University of California, San Diego, that the title of Luigi Palma di Cesnola's memoir *Ten Months in Libby Prison* had jumped out at me from the screen—most definitely a sign, from somewhere. Other wonderfully evocative names soon followed—Decimus et Ultimus Barziza, Giovanni Francesco Secchi de Casali, Tullio de Suzzara Verdi— names from a chapter of Italian American history which had been largely overlooked.

In recent years very important, often interdisciplinary, work has been done on this early phase or, as Robert Viscusi has called it, the "colonial" period of Italian American writing (44). As part of the growing attention to the multi-ethnic and multilingual character of the American literary tradition, an impressive number of previously obscure texts written in Italian, English, but also French and Spanish, by authors either born in Italy or of Italian descent, have been rescued from oblivion and justly reclaimed as part of what we call the Italian American heritage. I am thinking, in particular, of the precious findings in early Italian Americana we owe to Francesco Durante and Martino Marazzi.[1] More archival work can still be done, and new discoveries can be made, I am sure. Where, for example, is the English-language original of Tullio de Suzzara Verdi's 1894 *Vita Americana*?

Each new text added to the already impressive bibliography of Italian American primary sources belies the simplistic, dismissive categorization of this segment of American literary history as merely a rude testimony to immigration, a body of writing of more interest to the historian or the sociologist, than to the student of literature and culture. It is important to tell the whole story of Italian American literature, to trace its development and the ways in which it both reflects and illuminates the history of two

---

[1] See, for example, the wonderful two-volume anthology *Italian Americana*, edited by Durante, and Marazzi's monograph *Misteri di Little Italy*.

countries, as well as the formation of their complex, multi-faceted identities. The early Italian American writers, coming from a fragmented, foreign-ruled country with sharp distinctions between social classes, throw into bold relief, with their experiences and observations, the strengths and weaknesses of America's Democratic and Republican experiment. For Count Cesnola, for example, it is America's republicanism and (at least theoretical) egalitarianism, more than the initial language barrier, that make his adoptive country so foreign to him.

"Literature," as poet Dana Gioia has aptly put it, "is a conversation—between individuals, between generations, between cultures, between ages" (11) and over the years I have become keenly aware of this dialogue while moving back and forth between Anglo-American and Italian American writings. Returning to Sister Blandina Segale's memoir (and meeting with members of her order in Cicagna, her native town), after a period in which I had done research on the enormously popular anti-Catholic literature of the nineteenth century (some of which she mentions in her book), made me see more clearly than ever how some Italian American writers should be studied as part of America's religious history and faith-based writing which, as we know, played such a fundamental role in the making of American culture and identity. Sister Blandina's Catholicism informs her writing as deeply as Mary Rowlandson's Puritanism informed hers.

In my class on American modernism I have mentioned, as the perfect embodiment of that era's experimentalism, cosmopolitanism, and restlessness, the life and work of a self-styled "hurried man," Emanuel Carnevali, who literally re-invented himself (or, one might say, translated himself) as an American author in the early twentieth century. In a graduate seminar I conducted recently on the American family I included John Fante and placed his work alongside that of the much more canonical, but no less ethnic, Eugene O' Neill, because their explorations of family dynamics are similarly imbued with their cultural heritage and religious upbringing. Still one of the best-known names in the Italian American canon, Fante has also been justly recognized as a key figure in the literary portrayal of Southern California, more specifically Los Angeles (which also makes him part of twentieth-century American urban fiction), as well as in the rich American tradition of literature about the entertainment industry, inviting comparisons with Nathaniel West, Horace McCoy, John Steinbeck, Raymond Chandler, Budd Schulberg, and Francis Scott Fitzgerald.

A long time ago Fante and Jerre Mangione provided me with the material for a study of the anxiety-ridden relationship between authorship and masculinity in Italian American writing, a study which I first presented at an MLA convention, within the Division on Ethnic Studies in Language and Literature. In the cultural contexts in which Fante and Mangione grew up, spinning tales, creating art out of words was seen as woman's work, not that of a real man (Buonomo 61-73). And as I delved into their accounts of parental and community disapproval and distrust of their literary vocations, I could not help thinking back to the words and experience of a classic American writer from a very different time and place, but with strong ties to Italy: Nathaniel Hawthorne. Hawthorne thought of Italy as a "pleasant" land (less so, admittedly, after he actually set foot there), as a possible refuge from his utilitarian, practical-minded contemporaries to whom, no less than to his stern Puritan forebears as quoted in "The Custom House," the art of writing appeared frivolous, and of little service to mankind (142, 12). Hawthorne seemed to believe that many of his male contemporaries, fully engaged in, and committed to, trading, investing, exploring, building, would probably have joined his forefathers in their contemptuous assessment of his choice of profession: "the degenerate fellow might as well have been a fiddler!" (12). So would many in Fante's and Mangione's Italian American communities have done. Actually, to some of them being a fiddler would have seemed the more acceptable choice, because of the communal character of musical performance, as opposed to the solitary, "asocial" nature of writing.

Metaphorically disowned by patriarchs, Hawthorne turned to women, those "ladies conversant with" the mysteries of embroidery or, to be more specific, with the art of stitching letters on a piece of cloth, for they alone could fully understand the value of beauty (27). Similarly, in the books they imbued with their great love for language, both Fante and Mangione paid homage to those women storytellers in their families, who had set such a fine example to them with their respect for, and skillful handling of, words.

WORKS CITED

Boelhower, William. *Immigrant Autobiography in the United States: Four Versions of the Italian American Self.* Verona: Essedue Edizioni, 1982.

Barolini, Helen, ed. *The Dream Book: An Anthology of Writings by Italian American Women.* New York: Shocken Books, 1985.

Buonomo, Leonardo. *From Pioneer to Nomad: Essays on Italian North American Writing.* Toronto: Guernica, 2003.

Carnevali, Emanuel. *A Hurried Man.* Paris: Contact Editions, 1925.

Cesnola, Luigi Palma di. "Ten Months in Libby Prison." 1865. *From Pioneer to Nomad:* 23-36.

Durante, Francesco, ed. *Italoamericana: Storia e Letteratura degli italiani negli Stati Uniti 1776-1880.* Milano: Mondadori, 2001.

_______. *Italoamericana: Storia e Letteratura degli italiani negli Stati Uniti 1880-1943.* Milano: Mondadori, 2005.

Gioia, Dana. "Low Visibility: Thoughts on Italian American Writers." *Italian Americana* 12.1 (1993): 7-12.

De Suzzara Verdi, Tullio. *Vita Americana.* Trans. E. Arbib. Milano: Hoepli, 1894.

Hawthorne, Nathaniel. *The Scarlet Letter.* 1850. New York: W. W. Norton & Company, 1978.

Marazzi, Martino. *Misteri di Little Italy: Storie e testi della letteratura italoamericana.* Milano: Franco Angeli, 2001.

Segale, Sister Blandina. *At the End of the Santa Fe Trail.* 1932. Albuquerque: University of New Mexico Press, 1999.

Tamburri, Anthony Julian, Paolo A. Giordano, and Fred L. Guardaphé. *From the Margin: Writings in Italian Americana.* West Lafayette, IN: Purdue University Press, 1991.

Viscusi, Robert. "The History of Italian American Literary Studies." *Teaching Italian American Literature, Film, and Popular Culture.* Ed. Edvige Giunta and Kathleen Zamboni McCormick. New York: Modern Language Association of America, 2010. 43-58.

Graduate Studies, Italian American Literature, and the Humanities in the Twenty-first Century

Marina Camboni
University of Macerata

> I was a resident at the Bellagio center on Lake Como in Italy.... Lake Como branches into two arms, Lake Lecco to the east and the continuation of Como to the west. It was emblematic:.... I saw in the lakes the main body of who I am, American, and the Italian tributary.... From these two confluences I and my writing formed. My straddling position could be none other than that of the Italian American."
>
> —Helen Barolini

> Dream City ... is a place of many voices, where the unified singular self is an illusion.
>
> —Zadie Smith[1]

So many mental cells and creative energies were activated at the *Transcending Borders* Seminar in Bellagio that this final written contribution cannot but absorb the few facts and ideas I had brought to the meeting within the larger frame of the present forward-looking proposal. In my long experience as a teacher of American literature and director of a Ph.D. Program in Comparative Literature at the University of Macerata, Italian American literature has never been a specific object of study, either in American or comparative literature programs. Apart from the Master's thesis on Helen Barolini's, Tina de Rosa's, and Anna Quindlen's novels, which I tutored over the years, I date the beginning of my critical involvement at the time, about five years ago, when a Ph.D. student, Maria Giuseppina Cesari, asked me to tutor her work on third generation Italian American and Canadian novelists writing in English and French.[2]

[1] Quotations are taken from Helen Barolini's *Chiaroscuro* (128), and Zadie Smith's "Speaking in Tongues."

[2] Cesari, *Identità, memoria, mito e ritorno all'Italia nelle opere di tre autori nordamericani di origine italiana: Marco Micone, Nino Ricci e Don De Lillo*, Università degli Studi di Macerata 2011.

From: *Transcending Borders, Bridging Gaps* (Calandra Institute, 2015)

Through her I also met Fred Gardaphé, who became her informal co-tutor.

On account of my limited previous experience, my contribution will be programmatic, rather than illustrative. For, indeed, under the attentive supervision of Anthony Tamburri and the efficient coordination of Fred Gardaphé, two and a half days of furiously intense discussion were able to transform the initial cacophony of our individual and sectorial presentations into a more symphonically orchestrated and forward looking shared discourse. The IASN, our Transatlantic Network, with its agenda has provided both the blueprint for future common action, and the generative beginning of my reflections.

In the past couple of years, the most important economic paper in Italy, *Il sole 24 ore*, has been leading a campaign in support of culture and the humanities. A few months ago, two articles appeared there, side by side, under the common heading, "The Future of Humanities." The first, "Riappropriazione dei saperi," signed by the young narrator and Italianist Gabriele Pedullà, called for the recovery of a humanist perspective in the Humanities, in and out of the academic enclave; the second, "Ricreazione digitale," authored by the modern art historian Elena Giulia Rossi, reviewed *Umanistica Digitale*, an American book recently translated into Italian, where digital humanities is defined as a "global, holistic, trans-historic, and trans-medium approach, to learning and knowledge." (Burdick *et al.* 7).

Pedullà believes that we should recover the *spirit* and *values* of that "revolutionary intellectual movement that was Italian Humanism," and its most important contributions, the "perception of temporal distance," and "linguistic sensibility," i.e., attention to language and its potentialities. If the recovery of Humanism does not simply mean nostalgia for a time which saw Italy and the humanities influence all fields of learning in Europe, but stems from the recognition that many of the paradigmatic elements characterizing that phase of our history would still provide us with the mental frame we need to understand and interpret the human experience in our time, then we certainly need to recover it. A humanist *secularism*, and the value it put on *critical thinking*, are badly needed in today's world. The centrality given to the individual white western male and his agency, and the manifestly elitist structure of the humanist worldview, however, require critical re-examination. In addition, today's definition of what it means to be "human" must include the embodied, highly differentiated, and relational dimension of human existence, and the awareness of the role that culture, science and technology play in shaping our lives. As a result, studies in the humanities need to move beyond the hegemonic European and western, human-centered, perspective to build what can be paradoxically termed a *post human-centered humanism*, born out of the hard-learned lesson that humans are not the only living beings in the world; that our biosphere, sociosphere and semiosphere are interdependent systems, and that they must be integrated within the political projects and ethical structures of contemporary societies and cultures. This relational dimension also acknowledges the limits that the Cartesian paradigm we have inherited puts on our understanding of the world we experience and are part of (See Bennett; Damasio, 1994; Hayles, 1999).

Furthermore, in the twenty first century, humanist discourse cannot be centered on the settled citizen or farmer, and thus on a static and rooted subject, for its language and agency must also be built on a self caught in the dialectics of the need of stability and permanence, and the fluidity and uncertainty of lived life. This kind of self finds its referent, and symbol, in the uprooted migrant experience, which is creating a new subject of history and discourse (see Papastergiadis and Suárez-Orozco). The experience of migration admits difference as essential to its own construction; it acknowledges that relation and contact are central to the building of society, and that dialects and languages, including those of science and technology, like cultural texts and works of art, are not only goods to be coveted and horded to obtain and maintain power, but tools to be used to promote and develop new forms of transversal critical thinking, as classic Latin and Greek were for the Humanists. If computers and the web have become part of our extended mind, and memory, it is not so that we renounce our rights to think critically of and through them, and know what changes technology is bringing to our shared world. This New not-human-centered Humanism would be different from the Old Humanism, though it would definitely not be anti-human. Rather than a reappraisal of a specific, historically and culturally situated Italian Humanism, a New Humanism would, to quote a line from *ellis island*, "convey capacities humans have been refining since forever,"[3] in "a process of unending disclosure, discovery, self-criticism, and liberation" (Said 22).

Italian Humanism was built by individuals who created the semiotic works and texts on which it was grounded. The New Humanism has already produced its own model texts. I believe that Robert Viscusi's *ellis island* is one such text. I consider it also emblematic of the way Italian American literature is contributing to the building of our twenty-first century modernity. After all, *ellis island* is one of the outcomes of an experiment in teaching "method in the humanities" to contemporary American college students by a professor who wanted to pass on to them "two things: the art of making a good case in prose, and the art of investigating the traces of the past" (*ei* 319).

I descern a specific cultural sign of *Italianità* in Viscusi's humanist stance in *ellis island*.[4] A sign that is also highly visible in Helen Barolini's *Chiaroscuro*, where, telling of her education in a catholic school run by Irish nuns, she demarcates her Irish girl friend's catholicism from her own, which she describes as "skeptical, questioning, detached from ritual except in its aesthetic function" (13), "full of relativism and doubt, and *humanist* references" (14, emphasis added). In her attitude, we can descern the demotic humanism of heretical and popular Italian catholics who, in their distancing skepticism, suspected both political and ecclesiastical powers.

It is in this role as carrier and promoter of the kind of humanism we need in our globalized, polarized, capitalist-technological world, that I see the important, and unique, contribution of Italian American literary and artistic works. Italian American literature and cultural studies should not only be fully integrated within American, Italian, and comparative under-

---

[3] Book 10, sonnet 3, line 8. *ellis island* 2011, 56. Viscusi's epic poem is composed of fifty-two books of twelve sonnets of fourteen autonomous lines. From now on quotations from the volume will be abbreviated as *ei* followed by the numbers of book, sonnet, and line, as follows: 10.3: 8. *ei* simply followed by a numeral refers to page of the prose at the end of the volume.

[4] Agreeing with Piero Bassetti, in his introduction to *Re-reading Italian Americana*, Anthony J. Tamburri, pleads that critics of Italian American literature recognize "the Italian sign functions of that literature", p. X. I perceive in the recovery, or re-discovery, of the Humanist tradition one such sign. A sign that I believe would also help to connect one of the Italian American heroes, Christopher Columbus, not so much to the hegemonic history of conquest and colonization, as to the humanist tradition associating imagination and creativity to discovery and to an intellectual distancing from medieval tradition.

graduate and graduate studies in the university, but literary and artistic texts should be explored and studied by critics, becoming the material ground on which to base innovative critical theories and worldviews. As sociologist Pierre Bourdieu has amply demonstrated in his work on cultural capital, "literary production has to be approached in relational terms" and an understanding of a literary work "has to take into account everything which helps to constitute the work as such" (311, 317). Academic teaching and research are part of the collective literary, artistic, and cultural discourses which help constitute the "work as such," and transform it into a time-producing event.

I owe to Robert Viscusi's serendipitous gift of *ellis island* the revelation that, as creator of a world in connection, Italian American literature should have a paradigmatic role not only as 'minority' literature, but as a world relevant literature, on which to ground critical theory and literary studies. For, indeed, *ellis island*, a companion work to *Astoria*, can be considered the epic embodiment of the mass migration of Italians to the United States, re-visited by Viscusi as a paradigmatic model for what has "now become the typical life to be endured and decoded a million, a hundred million, times over" (*Astoria* 102).

In Viscusi's *ellis island* one can perceive how diasporas and migrations not only happen in time but in any given space produce a palimpsest of time-layers, where affinities and similarities as well as connecting nodes are made visible. While the node of different migrants/migrations meeting at the Ellis Island end of geographical space enhances the image of overlapping and contact of ethnic groups within a bound location, we must also imagine the separate threads wiring each individual or group to its land of origin, and the spreading out of smaller nodes connecting the island to the rest of the world. While in the past migration could be represented as a total uprooting and a one way journey from the home of origin to the new home, in today's gobalized world, the migrant must be perceived at once as the carrier of an interrupted story and the connector of lands, languages and cultures. As connector, the migrant becomes the agent, the subject, and the protagonist of a story of complex cultural circulation and transformation.

In his *Specimen Days* Walt Whitman respresented poetry as the place where historical time is incarnated. For him artists are "radiations" of poetry, the "furious whirling wheel," or vortex, that carries the present into the future:

> Comprehending artists in a mass, musicians, painters, actors, and so on, considering each and all of them as radiations or flanges of that furious whirling wheel, poetry, the centre and axis of the whole, where else indeed may we so well investigate the causes, growths, tallymarks of the time — the age's matter and malady? (872)

Alain Badiou, the French philosopher, must have taken Whitman's suggestion to heart, when in the book entitled *The Century* he investigated through poetry the "totalitarian" twentieth century (2), beginning his analysis with an in-depth reading of "Vek," the poem by Osip Mandelstam in which he detected a representation of the turning point and the junction of the nineteenth to the twentieth century.

By making Italian American emigration-immigration paradigmatic of the contemporary, collective, rather than individual, human experience of migration, Viscusi's *ellis island* joins the twentieth and the twenty-first centuries. Furthermore, as a text containing metatextual reflections, this epic also offers itself as a literary and aesthetic instantiation of contemporary culture.

Viscusi also seems to be adapting, and re-writing, Whitman's visionary representation of what moves humanity on, in the two two lines which begin section 2.7 of *ellis island*

> you have never seen a *human wheel turning*
> as it rolls heavily down the avenue of transformation
> (emphasis added)

While echoing Whitman's dynamic image for poetry and life, Viscusi transforms his "furious whirling wheel" into "a human wheel" whose downhill rolling represents the rapid transformation that comes with migration. It all begins with the decision to leave one's land of origin behind, for "[c]hoosing a life means boarding ship after a great hesitation full of suspense" (*ei* 22.8:10). Migration meaning uprooting and loss, it is no surprise that the poetry it generates is also "a tremendous blues of dispersal," whose "echoes keep changing languages in the colonnade" (*ei* 2.6:13,14).

"[R]emanet migratio nostra," writes Joseph Tusiani in his Latin poem "Ad Patrem," (250) meaning: migration is not a transitory event but an experience that displaces the memory of stability and permanence, inscribing over it one of dispersal, uncertitude, homelessness. And, if on the one hand, for Tusiani "the country I call my home / has now no home for me" ("The Soliloquy of Francis Vigo" 248), for John Ciardi, even the new country offers no real home. "I have a country but no town. / Home ran away from me," begins his "Talking Myself to Sleep at One More Hilton," which ends with the claim that the only place the persona in the poem can call home is "two shores / five hours apart, soon to be three. / And home is anywhere between." Home, then, has become the ocean itself.

Viscusi's *ellis island* recreates the world which begins with dislocation: the oceanic, watery world in which experiences follow one anoher, overlapping like ocean weaves. Weaves, and the ocean, on the other hand, provide the leading meaphors not only for the thought and narrative processes at work in the poem, but for time and succeeding migratory weaves.

In *ellis island* the single, autonomous, line with its compact unity of thought, image, and syntax, seems the formalized and linguistic incarnation of the "rupture" which is its theme. The single line is also the basic unit of the multiplying and combinatory algorhythm on which the web version of the epic is built.

Viscusi's epic is the work in which the epigraphic wisdom framed in a line, sculpted like a a proverb, provides the hard earned knowledge of migration. If Whitman celebrated "the self" in his "Song of Myself," Viscusi dramatizes the loss of that self—at once modern and American—and the multiplication of the voices, and languages, that inhabit that Italian, American, universal migrant self.

Ellis island is the allegory embodying the symbolic *home as liminal place* for those who are on the move, who have lost a home and cannot, or do not, want to find another on the old terms. While borrowing its name from a rock in the Bay of New York, (Viscusi could have named his poem *Lampedusa*, Italy, for that matter) the poem stands for what the American Ellis Island was not. It gives voice to the loss and the uprooting, the personal and cultural emotions connected with migration, thus providing the portrait of the twenty-first century subject-in-relation, a subject who is attached to other subjects, not only because it is part of the close-knit community of a town, village or nation, but because it is also involved in the world wide web of global interaction.

To this multiplied subject belongs a fluid text, a "Digital Humanities" text. "There are two kinds of text", Viscusi states in his website: "a printed text, which does not change, and an electronic text, which is in continuous process of random rearrangement," his *ellisislandpoem.com.*

If Humanism taught us to value classic and ancient languages, Digital Humanism makes us aware of the other languages critics and writers have at their disposal in this globalized and web-connected world. It makes us aware of the web of texts in which we are enmeshed and underscores the absence of those cancelled from history, texts that will never contribute to shape us, unless we recognize their value and recover them. It also interrogates human centrality together with authority and authoriality, and what kind of freedom, what kind of society humans can build (see Hayles 2012).

This is exactly what *ellisisland.com*, in many ways, does. Like an island, or node, in the sea of the web, this work can be reached, and appropriated, by a wide range of people from all nations, women and men, native speakers of different languages. As a fluid text, however, it is never the same, for, with one click, a sonnet is produced which has no equivalent in the printed text, being the random association of lines from different sonnets. Sonnets, however, are produced one at the time. Thus the surfer of the web, who cannot form an overall picture of the epic, has complete freedom to create his own epic by copying and pasting together the poems that appear on the computer screen, click after click.

The questions that such a web-based text poses to the reader and critic are, like migration, the outcome of a number of losses that combine with the loss of human centrality: certainty of authoriality; stability of sense and meaning; singularity of story and identity; differenciated roles of writer and reader. How do we read and interpret such texts? Can we engage in in-depth readings or hermeneutical interpretations of computer-generated texts? Can we still use the word "text" for writing that a machine has generated?

We have been taught to search for intention and author-created meanings in literary texts. Freud and psychoanalysis has made us aware of what authors unconsciously—and readers consciously and unconsciously—contribute to apparently finished texts. But what do we know about algo-rhythmically created texts, and about chance occurrences? How do we deal with chance and change?

If the Italian migration to the United States provides the paradigm of twentieth century modernity, Viscusi's epic poem provides the cultural text from which to infer our twenty-first century interrogations but also hints at what needs to be changed in our ethic and epistemological paradigms. His story is neither one, nor whole, it is rather a collection of multiple, fragmented stories, for "you are not a story but an aspect of a story's story" (1.3:10). These stories not only multiply but, as in the first book of the epic, "disintegrate you like waves." (1.3:3). Between them all, however, the stories form the narratives that weave together the individual ("contradiction and conflict weave you together anew in every living moment" *ei* 10.3:9) and the communities, the twentieth century and the twenty-first century.

These multiple stories are the familiar turf for twenty first century *digital natives.* With his printed *ellis island* and fluid *ellisisland.com*, Viscusi has not only created the *New Italian American Epic*, but offered an emblematic Italian American text, and an example of why Italian American Studies in the academy can provide an important contribution to the building of contemporary literary and cultural discourse. Through the joint effort of Italian and American scholars and students, Italian American Studies can create a shared canon of authors and critics and, also thanks to Digital Humanities, reappropriate the Italian and Italian American Cultural Heritage both to build memory and identity, and to create theoretical and critical models shaping a New Humanism in the age of technology.

WORKS CITED

Badiou, Alain. *Being and Event*. London: Continuum 2006.

Barolini, Helen. *Chiaroscuro: Essays of Identity*. Madison: Wisconsin P, 1999.

Bennett, Jane. *Vibrant Matter: A Political Echology of Things*. Durham, NC: Duke UP, 2010.

Bourdieu, Pierre. "The Field of Cultural Production, or: The Economic World Reversed." *Poetics* 12 (1983): 311-356.

Burdick, Anne, Johanna Drucker, Peter Lunenfeld, Todd Presner and Jeffrey Schnapp. *Digital_Humanities*. Cambridge, MA: MIT Press 2012.http://mitpress.mit.edu/sites/default/files/titles/content/9780262018470_Open_Access_Edition.pdf.

Ciardi, John. "Talking Myself to Sleep at One More Hilton." *The Atlantic Monthly* (April 1966): 81.

Damasio, Antonio. *Descartes' Error: Emotion, Reason, and the Human Brain*. New York: Putnam Publishing 1994.

Hayles, Katherine. *How We Became Posthuman: Virtual Bodies in Cybernetics, Literature, and Informatics*. Chicago: U Chicago P, 1999.

______. *How We Think: Digital Media and Contemporary Technogenesis*. Chicago: U Chicago P, 2012.

Papastergiadis, Nikos. *The Turbulence of Migration*. Oxford: Blackwell 2000.

Pedullà, Gabriele. "Riappropriamoci dei saperi." *Il Sole 24 Ore* 115 (27 April 2014): 30.

Rossi, Giulia Elena. "Ricreazione digitale." *Il Sole 24 Ore* 115 (27 April 2014): 30.

Said, Edward W. *Humanism and Democratic Criticism*. Palgrave McMillan 2004.

Smith, Zadie. "Speaking in Tongues." *The New York Review of Books* 56.3 (February 2009).

Suárez-Orozco, Marcelo M. "Everything You Ever Wanted to Know About Assimilation But Were Afraid to Ask." *The New Immigration: An Interdisciplinary Reader*. Marcelo M. Suárez-Orozco, Carola Suárez-Orozco, and Desirée Baolian Qin, eds. New York and London: Routledge 2005. 67-83.

Tamburri, Anthony Julian. *Re-reading Italian Americana: Specificities and Generalities on Literature and Criticism*, Plymouth, Fairleigh Dickinson UP, 2014.

Tusiani, Joseph. "Ad Patrem" and "The Soliloquy of Francis Vigo." In Anthony Julian Tamburri, Paolo A. Giordano, and Fred Gardaphé, eds. *From the Margin: Readings in Italian Americana*. 2nd Edition. West Lafayette: Purdue UP, 2000. 250, 248.

Viscusi, Robert. *Astoria*. Toronto-New York: Guernica 1995.

______. *ellis island*. New York: Bordighera Press 2011; *ellisislandpoem.com*.

Whitman, Walt. "Specimen Days." *Complete Poetry and Prose*. Justin Kaplan, ed. New York: The Library of America 1982.

Italian Immigrant Literary Studies in the U.S. An Orphan Child?

Paul Giordano
University of Central Florida

Except for a few pages on Helen Barolini's *Umbertina*, and a few other Italian American writers born in the United States who expressed themselves in English, I have, in the past, strictly dealt with Italian immigrant writers. In Italian-American Studies my name is mostly tied to Joseph Tusiani, having written a number of articles on his poetry and the autobiographical trilogy, *La parola difficile, La parola nuova,* e *La parola antica*. I have also worked on Italian writers who addressed the issue of emigration and who gave us the perspective of those who remained behind, and the hardships that emigration wrought on Italian families and frequently on whole villages and towns: Some of the texts that come to mind are *Sull'Oceano* by Edmondo de Amicis which gives us a first-hand account of what it was like to cross the ocean in steerage; Giovanni Pascoli's poem "Italy," dedicated to a theme dear to Pascoli, that Italian emigrants forced painfully to abandon their home to seek a better life in another country; Luigi Pirandello's "L'altro figlio," a short story from his collection *Novelle per un anno,* and popularized by the Taviani brothers in their film *Kaos*; Rodolfo di Biasio's short novel *I quattro camminanti*, a novel derived from the hundreds of letters that four brothers, the "quattro camminanti" of the title mailed, over the years, to their mother in Italy.[1]

Given my research preferences I was really quite pleased when I received my assignment for the Bellagio conference—"Italian Immigrant Literary Studies in the U.S.: An Orphan Child?" Italian immigrant writing is a topic that is central to my research interests.

The quick and very short answer to the question posed to me is a resounding YES, Italian Immigrant writing has, until recently, been

[1] For further information on Italian writers and emigration see: De Nicola, Francesco. *Gli scrittori italiani e l'emigrazione* (FormiaL Ghenoma s.r.l.).

From: *Transcending Borders, Bridging Gaps* (Calandra Institute, 2015)

almost forgotten. These foundational texts are not read and are not taught in the various classes and programs of Italian and Italian-American studies in the U.S. One of the reasons for the current state of affairs is that most of the books from this early period are out of print and not available. Just as important, do scholars and teachers of Italian and Italian-American Studies literature think that these writers are important to the "program"?

These thousands of novels, poems, plays, biographies, autobiographies, journals, dailies and other forms of expression written in Italian are important, amazingly so, if we want to fully understand the migration experience and the formation, or creation, of an "Italian-American" identity or, more accurately, identities. As a number of the colleagues present at the Bellagio conference/workshop pointed out, we are not a homogenous group. Our experiences are different. Of the nine colleagues present that came from the United States three emigrated to the United States between 1957 and 1963, two emigrated much later, and four are second and third generation Italian-American. We all have different experiences and, I venture to say, we all have lived, and live our hyphenated identity differently.[2]

Mary Jo Bona wrote, "Perhaps it is our fortune that we do not possess a single definition of ourselves." To expand and complete the definition of "ourselves" we need to look at the whole picture and, obviously, that includes the writings of our Italian immigrant forebears.

Throughout the nineteenth and twentieth century the myth of America attracted millions of Italians to its shore, among them literary critics, mainstream writers and intellectuals. Some came for short visits and wrote about their travels and perceptions, though limited they may have been. Among them, the literary critic Emilio Cecchi's *America amara,* the futurist Fortunato Depero's *Un futurista a New York* (notes published posthumously), Mario Soldati's *America primo amore*, and Goffredo Parise's *Odore d'America* come to mind. Others, like Giuseppe Prezzolini, stayed longer and their impact was more lasting. Giuseppe Prezzolini, Professor of Italian at Columbia University and director of its Casa Italiana, was a mis-

[2] Fred L, Gardaphé's "Identical Difference: Notes on Italian and Italian-American Identities," in *The Essence of Italian Culture and the Challenge of a Global Age. Cultural Heritage and Contemporary Change*. Ed. George McClean and Piero Bassetti Series IV, West Europe (Series IV, West Europe, Volume 5) (The Council for Research in Values and Philosophy, 2003) 93-112.

sionary of Italian culture and a highly respected intellectual who, during his stay in America wrote, among other things, *I trapiantati* (1953), *America in pantofole* (1950), *America con gli stivali* (1954) and an interesting article "America and Italy: Myths and Realities." (*Italian Quarterly* [Spring 1959]).

Along with these Italian literati, a generation of writers, journalists, playwrights, political and religious activists and exiles emigrated whose purpose was to make the New World their home. Bernardino Ciambelli (1862–1931) was a journalist, author of novels and plays, and also an actor and "capocomico." His novels not only tell stories about Italian immigrants they also describe the city of New York at the end of the 19th century and the first decades of the 20th: the undergrounds, the multi-ethnic neighborhoods, Chinatown, The Irish brothels, Little Italy, and other details of life.[3] Samuel Charles Mazzuchelli, O.P. (1806–1864) a pioneer Italian Catholic missionary who brought the church to the Iowa-Illinois-Wisconsin tri-state area. He founded a number of parishes in the area, and was the architect for a number of parish buildings. Among his many contributions, Mazzucchelli translated a catechism into the Winnebago language, and published an almanac in the Chippewa language. Pasquale (Pascal) D'Angelo came to the United States at the age of 16. While working as a laborer and living under brutal conditions he taught himself English and began to write poetry. Soon his poems were published in important literary journals such as *The Literary Review*, *The Nation*, and *The New York Times*. In 1924, he published his autobiography *Son of Italy*[4] where this "pick and shovel" worker, as he describes himself, narrates the harsh, almost inhumane, conditions that he and other immigrants suffered. Riccardo Cordiferro, baptized Alessandro Sisca, was a poet, essayist, playwright, historical scholar, anarchist who spent a number of years in jail for his political activity. He was the founder of *La Follia di New York*, a magazine whose life spanned a century, and the author of a popular Neapolitan song, "Core 'ngrato." These are but a few examples of the many

[3] See Francesco Durante's interview in the magazine, *We the Italians* published October 24, 2013.

[4] D'Angelo, Pascal (Pasquale). *Son of Italy: the autobiography of Pascal D'Angelo*, recently re-published by Guernica Press

that are documented in Rose Basile Green's groundbreaking work *The Italian-American Novel*[5] and Francesco Durante's monumental *Italoamericana: The Literature of the great Migration 1880-1943.*[6]

Beginning with the nineteen-nineties we have witnessed the beginning of a fertile period for the scholarship of the early period of Italian immigrant writing. Francesco Durante, journalist for "Il mattino" of Naples and Professor at the University Suor Orsola Benincasa published an enormous two volume critical study and anthology titled *Italoamericana* published by Mondadori: the first tome is about the literature of Italians that emigrated to the U.S.A. from 1776 to 1880 (2001); the second book deals with the literature of the period that spans the "great migration" from 1880 and 1943 (2005). This second volume was translated and published by Fordham University Press this past year. Durante's monumental study was followed by two excellent studies by Martino Marazzi, *Voices of Italian America* and *A occhi aperti: letteratura dell'emigrazione e mito Americano.*[7] Marazzi's studies trace the cultural history of Italian immigrants during the first half of the twentieth century and offer the reader a path to understanding the fabrication of Italian-American history and culture. As important as the historical, and literary and cultural analysis is, the most valuable contribution of Marazzi's book is the anthology, which gave new life to the works of numerous writers that most of us have not read and most likely had never heard their names. To these ground breaking studies we must add Ilaria Serra's study *The Value of Worthless Lives s*[8] that, for the first time, explores the "mostly unpublished, often thickly accented, tales of ordinary men and women . . . to reflect (their) realities of work, survival, identity, and change." To these studies, one must also include Jim Pericone's excellent annotated bibliography *Strangers in a Strange Land. A*

---

[5] Basile-Green, Rose. *The Italian American Novel: An Interaction of Two Cultures* (Madison, NJ: Fairleigh Dickenson University Press, 1974).

[6] Durante, Francesco. *Italoamericana: The Literature of the great Migration 1880-1947* (Milano: Mondadori, 2005).

[7] Marazzi, Martino. *Voices of Italian America: A History of Early Italian American Literature with a Critical Anthology* (Fordham University Press, 2011) and *A occhi aperti: letteratura dell'emigrazione e mito American* (Milano: Franco Angeli Editore 2011).

[8] Serra, Ilaria. *The Value of Worthless Lives: Writing Italian Immigrant Autobiographies* (New York: Fordham University Press, 2007).

Survey of Italian-language American Imprints (1830–1945). This wonderful book catalogues the Italian-language book-publishing industry that began in the nineteenth century and flourished in the United States in the fifty years before World War II.[9]

This early period comes to an end in the years immediately following World War II. As Martino Marazzi states in the above mentioned *Voices of Italian America,* "The Italian-America that speaks and writes Italian, or its dialects, in the literary sense has disappeared forever." One could say that this period ends with Joseph Tusiani,[10] one of the last of this group who with eloquence and dignity addressed the experience of immigration to the United States in his Italian-American trilogy written in Italian, *La parola difficile, La parola nuova* and *La parola antica*, with the collective subtitle *Autobiografia di un italo-americano.* In the 958 pages of the trilogy, Tusiani not only narrates his life and that of his family from the day he landed in New York in 1947, he also takes us on a voyage through the history of Italian migration to the United States. Many of the people, some famous others not, that grace the pages of this work constitute the essence of this migration.[11]

Since the 1950s we have witnessed a second wave of writers from Italy who produced, and continue to produce a substantial amount of poetry and prose both in the Italian language and in the English language. The list is long: Joseph Tusiani, Giose Rimanelli, Peter Carravetta, Gianna Patriarca, Frances Winwar (Francesca Vinciguerra) Luigi Fontanella, Paolo Valesio, Luigi Ballerini, Rita Dinale, Alessandro Carrera, and Emanuele Pettener are some of the more prominent names. Through their writing a distinctive American voice in Italian literature, or maybe an Italian voice

---

[9] Periconi, James J., *Strangers in a Strange Land. A Survey of Italian-language American Imprints (1830-1945* (New York: Bordighera Press, 2013).

[10] See Marazzi's., *Voices of Italian America* (2011) and my "Tra autobiografia e romanzo: Il sogno italo-americano. Realtà e immaginario dell'emigrazione negli Stati Uniti. *Atti del Convegno "Il sogno italo-americano" 28-30 novembre 1996.* A cura di Sebastiano Martelli (Napoli: Suor Orsola Benincasa, 1998) 89-108.

[11] Tusiani, Joseph, *La Parola Difficile Autobiografia di un italo-americano* (Bari: Schena Editore, 1988); *La Parola Nuova Autobiografia di un italo-americano* (Bari: Schena Editore, 1991); *La Parola Antica Autobiografia di un italo-americano* (Bari: Schena Editore, 1992).

in American literature is starting to define itself. These writers have given a new voice to Italian America, and, by their form and content, they give recognition to the fact that Italian America is neither monolingual nor monocultural.[12] Unfortunately, many of these books suffered the same fate as those of their predecessors and quickly went out of print.

The studies mentioned above have given us a clearer understanding of the literary production and cultural history of that period of mass migration and indicate a path to follow. We now also have a book, Marazzi's *Voices of Italian America* that can be used as a text in a university course on early Italian immigrant writing. What is needed now is to build on these studies and, more importantly, create a curriculum to bring this information to the classroom, if not, this knowledge will continue to remain the domain of the few. To bring this knowledge to our students a conscientious effort is needed to rescue these writings from the dustbin of history and find a way to have at least a number of these books re-published in the original Italian and translated into English, either in traditional book form or digitized. This, as many of you know, is a long and tedious process and for anything to be accomplished one needs grant money, time and a team of scholars to work on it together, I am also thinking of graduate students who could turn some of this work into dissertations and publications. I have begun working with the Digital Humanities Center at my university to see what can be done, what roads to take and what strategies to develop.

Giuseppe Prezzolini was quoted as saying that Italian immigrants left behind tears and sweat but not words, living their lives in America mostly in silence, their memories private and stories untold. The studies that have

---

[12] See Anthony Julian Tamburri's Editor's Note and Peter Carravetta's "Concept, Direction, Introduction" to "Poessay VI: Voices from the Italian Diaspora." in *Romance Language Notes* II (1991): 13-15. Also Paolo Valesio's excellent introduction to *Poesaggio: Poeti italiani d'america.* Eds. Peter Carravetta & Paolo Valesio (Quinto di Treviso: Pagus, 1993). On Italian writers in America see also Anthony Julian Tamburri, "Identità 'italiana': Ovvero lo scrittore italiano all'estero." *Meditations on Identity - Meditazioni su identità.* Ed. Anthony Julian Tamburri (New York: Bordighera Press, 2014) 51- 64; Fontanella, Luigi. *La Parola Trasfuga* (Fiesole: Edizioni Cadmi, 2003); and my "Emigrants, Expatriates and/or Exiles: Italian Writing in America." *Beyond the Margin: Further Writings in Italian Americana.* Eds. Paul A. Giordano and Anthony Julian Tamburri (Rutheford, NJ: Fairleigh Dickinson University Press, December 1997) 223-241.

been published in the recent past prove Prezzolini wrong, but unless we bring this wealth of knowledge to the classroom and disseminate it to our students and to a more general public, these voices will once again descend into oblivion.

Italian American Literature in/and the Canon
The Question of Teaching

Donatella Izzo
University of Naples, "L'Orientale"

i was reading the story of stories of stories
they tell on the walls of ellis island
the stories disintegrate you like waves

they break you into a thousand thousand faces
looking out at the skyline from the ships
which of them do you become . . .

you are the eyes that transform the city
giving it the softness of napoli

—Robert Viscusi, *Ellis Island*, 1.3

The experience I will attempt to share in these few notes is an experience of situated teaching—or rather, an experience of situated non-teaching: my own failure to teach Italian American literature, largely due to my students' deeply ingrained and repeatedly expressed lack of interest in all things Italian American. Over the twenty years I have spent teaching at my university, not once has Italian American literature, or an Italian American author, been mentioned in response to the question "topics or texts you'd like to find in next year's course" in my end-of-year questionnaires. In all those years of teaching, and I don't know how many hundreds of BA and MA theses supervised, only three times have I had requests for thesis topics in Italian American literature: one on Mario Puzo's *The Godfather*, one on Don DeLillo's *Underworld*, and one on DeLillo's *Point Omega*—and the latter explicitly originated in an interest in the philosophical implications of contemporary literature, rather than the ethnicity of the novel's author.

This lack of interest might perhaps be perceived as normal elsewhere in the country, but it appears somewhat puzzling in light of the fact that I teach at Università di Napoli "L'Orientale," and the overwhelming majority of my students come from Campania and the rest of Southern Italy,

From: *Transcending Borders, Bridging Gaps* (Calandra Institute, 2014)

that is, the area that accounts for eighty percent of the five million Italians who migrated to the United States of America between 1876 and 1930. Admittedly, that was over a century ago, and memories of uncles and cousins who moved to the States may be less vivid for my students' generation than they were in my own family as I was growing up; but still, many of my students have relatives in the United States that they regularly visit, and one would expect them to feel a connection to and an interest in the culture of that community. And yet, personal connection is one thing and intellectual interest is another: indeed, as I will argue in the notes that follow, under certain circumstances the two may even be at odds. But let me not get ahead of myself.

In trying to account for the virtual disappearance of Italian Americans from our objects of study, I will propose two orders of explanation—one wider and more institutional in kind, and the other more specific, which I would define as socio-psychological. I will then relate the responses to a questionnaire that I recently submitted to some of my students and former students, whose results, I believe, offer some food for thought and yield some answers and perhaps hope for the future.

The wider order of explanation, of course, has to do with the structure of Italian academia itself, especially as regards the study of American literature. When they start university, most Italian students have had no opportunity of becoming acquainted with U.S. literature, since the high school curriculum, where it includes a foreign literature, is overwhelmingly based on the British classics. That means we have to build up from scratch—sometimes over a three-year span, sometimes in just one year, almost invariably counting on just one course a year—a basic knowledge of American literary history and of its texts and authors. Such a task leaves little time to explore the many articulations of American literature, especially those that haven't made it into the canon, however broadly one may want to define it.

This institutional difficulty is compounded by the training of many of us teachers. As Americanists educated outside of the United States in the days before the multicultural explosion, many of us have been trained to believe that our main task as scholars was appropriating a knowledge of canonical Anglo-American literature, and to reject the idea of pursuing a career in Italian American studies—something that we would perceive not just as marginal to the field imaginary, but also as suspiciously based on our privileged insider knowledge of the Italian culture, and thus liable to keep us locked in the role of "native informants" rather than enabling us to access the wider field on equal intellectual terms. This emphasis on mainstream U.S. culture as "the real thing," issuing from and reflecting the hegemonic cultural experience of the United States, is frequently mirrored not just in our teaching practice, but also in the students' spontaneous hierarchization between canonical and "ethnic" experience, based not on direct knowledge of either but on their relative positions in an ideal gamut of cultural options where "ethnic" stands for marginal and particular rather than dominant and universal, and thus enjoys a relatively lower status. While many of us have of course worked to challenge and complicate such a mono-cultural perception of the U.S. literary landscape, the institutional constraints are such that the general framework of our teaching, especially at BA level, still tends to be very much what David Palumbo-Liu denounced in his 1995 *The Ethnic Canon*, with all but the most established African American literary landmarks still invisible, or else inserted into the syllabus in ways that enlarge and complement, but do not seriously undermine the assumed priority of the mono-cultural competence and standards. (Let me also note in passing that even this very bland multicultural move is not without its risks in such an institutionally—although, luckily, not intellectually—conservative educational system as the Italian one. Even the American canon is still widely considered inferior as compared with the British and European classics, and until a few years ago, students taking a degree in American instead of British literature were not allowed to embrace a career as high school teachers).

In this context, Italian American literature seems to struggle under a double stigma. On the one hand, aesthetic prejudice, the ethnic being traditionally associated with a realistic rendering of the immigrant experience rather than modernist paradigms of literary value—complex and universal worldview, formal experiment, and stylistic sophistication. In the particular case of Italian American literature, its aesthetic quality may be further overshadowed by a twofold standard of literary excellence—not just the paradigm associated with the modern U.S. canon but also the one associated with the Italian classics. On the other hand, political prejudice: unlike other "ethnic" fields, Italian American studies is not perceived as directly connected to a strong civil rights movement, as are African American studies, Native American studies, Asian American studies, and Latino/Latina studies. Of course, this impression is partly the result of a form of historical myopia—one need only think of Sacco and Vanzetti to realize that, if anything, the radical political commitment of Italian Americans antedated the political movements of the 1960s and 1970s that ushered in the so called "culture of dissensus." But this does not change the fact that, today, there seems to be no immediately visible political stake or counter-hegemonic value in focusing on the literary and cultural tradition of a racially unmarked, successfully assimilated community—nothing that can effectively mobilize what Liam Kennedy has defined "the romance or fetishization of the trope of race in European studies of American culture" (574). In short, as an object of study Italian American literature is simultaneously perceived as not *canonical* enough and not *political* enough: not quite/not white, to misappropriate Homi Bhabha's famous expression.

Apart from its peculiar position within the academic world, another broad factor that apparently contributes to limiting the potential appeal of Italian American literature in the eye of students is its scarce mediatic circulation and scanty visibility on the Italian publishing market, with very few exceptions—John Fante, Don DeLillo, and Mario Puzo's *The Godfather*. I believe that my students' responses to the questionnaire I circulated among them are fairly representative in this respect.[1] The first two questions were "Have you ever read any Italian American author?" and "Whether you have read them or not, could you mention the name of any Italian American author?" Of the sixteen students who replied to the questionnaire, eight had never read any Italian American author, and four among these could not even name any. Of the remaining eight, four declared that they had read Don DeLillo (two of them had actually written their thesis about one of his novels, as I mentioned before), two had read John Fante, and two did not specify which author they had read. Among the fourteen students who were able to name one or more Italian American authors, eight mentioned Don DeLillo, five each John Fante and Lawrence Ferlinghetti, four Mario Puzo, three Gregory Corso, two Gay

[1] The questionnaire, comprising five questions and soliciting responses on a free and voluntary basis, was submitted by e-mail on January 26, 2014 to 136 BA and MA students and former students. Only 16 responded—an unusually low percentage compared with other previous experiences, and one that might be taken to reflect their relative lack of interest in the topic. The questionnaire was in Italian; the English translation of the students' responses is mine.

Talese (one mentioning him as "a guy who has written about the Mafia"), two Christopher Paolini, one Linda Kenney Baden, and finally, one Pietro Di Donato's *Christ in Concrete*. Interestingly, few of these names seem to be directly connected to the Italian American experience: DeLillo is prevalently perceived as an ethnically unmarked contemporary writer (three out of four of the students who had actually read one or more of his works explicitly underscored that they found little or no connection to Italian Americanness there); Corso and Ferlinghetti (whom none of the students had read) benefit from the popularity of the Beat Generation (and Ferlinghetti probably also from a recent exhibition of his paintings at the National Archeological Museum in Naples); Baden and Paolini produce popular bestsellers as the authors, respectively, of a thriller novel series and of a fantasy saga, the *Eragon* tetralogy. Of the writers mentioned, probably only Fante and Di Donato are clearly identifiable as unequivocally Italian American in both ethnicity and subject matter, as well as being major literary figures.

Equally revealing are the responses to my third question, "What do you know about the Italian American community? What are the main sources of your information? To which images or characteristics is it associated in your mind?" In this case, only three out of sixteen students declare that they have no knowledge whatsoever of the Italian American community; one student has an uncle's family in New Jersey, and offers observations about the relative impact of class and generation in defining the Italianness of the Italian American community, while also underlining the gap between the latter and its stereotyped representation in movies and TV shows. The overwhelming majority, on the other hand, mention the historical experience of Italians in the United States as generally poor, illiterate, and discriminated immigrants, or else the present-day representation of Italian Americans as stereotyped characters in movies and TV shows, or both. Many express their uneasiness with the representation of Italian Americans in such shows as *Jersey Shore* or *The Sopranos*, and virtually all manifest their troubled awareness that their knowledge of the community is filtered through heavy, sometimes parodic, frequently offensive stereotyping.

I believe that this generalized awareness of both the community's discriminated past and its stereotyped present can go some way towards explaining what I called, at the beginning of these notes, my students' deeply ingrained and repeatedly expressed lack of interest in all things Italian American—a lack of interest which may be only apparent and which, upon reflection, I would rather define as a veritable resistance. Let me now move to what I earlier defined the socio-psychological part of my considerations. I will do so by way of an anecdote.

A few years ago, in 2009, I took a group of my American literature students on a two-week trip to the United States. Among the places of interest we visited was the Ellis Island Immigration Museum. As is well known, the Museum offers access to a genealogical database where visitors can look up their family name and find matches in immigration records. Every single one of my students looked up their name, and not one of them failed to find it. This was hardly surprising, after all, considering the immigration rate from the region we all came from. And yet, however predictable, this little episode came as a shock of recognition to many of them, offering sudden embodied evidence of vaguely heard family stories, and creating connections where previously there had been none.

For me, too, this episode came as something of a shock of recognition. These students, enthralled by the sudden realization that people actually or potentially related to themselves had once crossed the ocean and probably had progeny that was even now living somewhere in the United States, grandchildren and great-grandchildren that might very well have been *them* under different circumstances—these students, I thought, were the same students who when asked about what they would like to find in next year's syllabus never once mentioned Italian American literature or a single Italian American author. Perhaps, I thought, this lack of interest was not due simply to the relative obscurity of the Italian American tradition within the landscape of American Studies at large—after all, as we have seen, there is nothing obscure to Don DeLillo, John Fante, or Lawrence Ferlinghetti. What suddenly dawned on me, and what I have been verifying in the course of numerous conversations, is that what motivated such a disconnection between ethnicity and academic investment was not so much a lack of curiosity as a deep-seated resistance. By going into American Studies they had chosen an object that was other than them, an object that was (seen as) thoroughly modern, supposedly more cosmopolitan, more globally influential, and more advanced. What Ellis Island revealed was the split between the America they were seeking and the America, but also the Italy, that the Italian American experience mirrored back at them: a place which led many of them back to a darker time of class subalternity and racial discrimination, from which their ancestors had struggled to emerge, and with which they were now called to identify themselves—the very past that their education was supposed to emancipate them from.

This uneasiness, I suspect, is not just past-oriented. One student, immediately after relating in the questionnaire what she had learnt about the conditions of poverty, social marginalization, and racism faced by Italian immigrants of old in the American ghettoes, added a final sentence: "More recent immigration is definitely different, certainly connected to study and research." A revealing enough sentence. While forging a perhaps unwanted connection to a devalued familial and regional past, an exploration of the Italian American experience can also induce anxiety over a quite possible future. Especially in such a place as Naples, students are well aware of how, as twenty-first century young intellectuals preparing to go on the job market in the middle of the worst job crisis of the last century, they might soon be sharing the experience of their ancestors, albeit in a new key. Hence, my suspicion that their contradictory attitude to Italian America may be the result of a complex play of intersecting identifications and dis-identifications.

If that is so, the question—at least as far as the specific teaching situation I have tried to outline—is finally not so much one of putting Italian American literature back into the U.S. literary canon, but rather one of reconfiguring the paradigms according to which Italian American literature may become relevant without becoming threatening, and operate as a field where historical issues may display a new cogency, and present-day issues can be explored in their historical depth. My students' responses to the questionnaire once again provide suggestions. When asked to place a list of U.S. literary traditions in order of personal preference as potential objects of study,[2] eight students placed the literary canon first as imperative and irreplaceable, four African American literature as (one student writes) "a parallel canon," and four Italian American literature, which furthermore

[2] The question was: "If you could choose the topics/writers to be found in your American literature syllabus, which literary tradition or group of authors/texts would you choose? Please list them in order of preference and explain why." The traditions were, in alphabetical order: African American, Asian American, Italian American, Jewish American, Latino/a, Literary mainstream/Literary canon.

ranks second in five cases—a good ranking but still one that clearly reflects the perceived (and received) hierarchy within the field. However, when stepping outside of a comparative framework, the students are asked whether they would like to study Italian American literature more systematically and in depth, all but one respond in an eager affirmative, as if they had suddenly been shocked into an awareness of their lack.[3] One student writes: "I had never realized my ignorance about this topic before I filled out this questionnaire." The reasons adduced for this newly realized interest are diverse: curiosity for a topic one has heard little about; an interest in accessing the human experience the literature portrays, going beyond the stereotype; an interest in getting a more complete view of how the U.S. treats its ethnic minorities; a view of Italian American literature as a bridge between the two cultures, and an expression of the Italian view of the United States; a wish to know more about how Italian culture has developed in the United States, about Italian American literature as a modern tradition branching out from Italian literature, and about Italian American history as "a branch of our very Italian history," as one student writes; a wish to understand the operation, respectively, of the microcosm and the macrocosm across the national boundaries. Other students more clearly speak to their prospective migrant condition and to contemporary global concerns: "As an Italian, I think it would be interesting to know more about the Italian American community. I also believe that this knowledge can be more easily and 'naturally' spent internationally and generally in a global context. Each scholar's cultural specificity should, I believe, inform the scholar's participation in and contribution to the supranational academic debate." Another student—the same one who had mentioned intellectual migration in a previous reply—writes:

> Finally, I think this phenomenon is indirectly relevant to our generation, as well, since I believe we all more or less have some relative who migrated to America, whether he stayed there or came back, or have heard such stories from our grandparents or their friends. And so, in a way, this also speaks a little to what we have become. One more thing: beyond the aca-

[3] Question four: "If you were able to choose the topics or authors of your American literature syllabus, would you be interested in studying the literature, the cultural tradition, and the socio-historical experience of the Italian American community? If so, why? If not, why?"

> demic context, reflecting on Italian emigration wouldn't hurt, these days, given the spread of racism in Italy, migrants' boats coming ashore, immigrant detention centers, etc.—maybe this is an old rhetoric, but....

I believe this range of responses can help us find a key to updating and shifting our paradigms. Rather than thinking in terms of Italian American literature and the U.S. canon, or even the U.S. "ethnic canon," the potential recipients of our future courses are thinking outside the box of the nation—mainly because they conceive themselves as being, willy-nilly, outside that box. To them, the literary tradition—much as their prospective future as forced members of a globalized intellectual labor—is simultaneously rooted in a cultural identity and deterritorialized, enabling a range of comparative, infra-, inter-, and trans-national frameworks that is exactly mirrored by their plural representations of Italian American literature as being at once an extension of Italian literature, part of American literature, and one of a plurality of diasporic traditions across the globe. Their ancestors' migration is reconfigured not so much in terms of a historically given, U.S.-oriented assimilation trajectory, but rather as the historical antecedent of an ongoing global diaspora, a migration flow which may and indeed does constantly involve them in manifold roles—simultaneously as privileged citizens and as themselves more or less disenfranchised migrants. In their clear-headed look on the connections stretching from their ancestors' past to their own present and future, and in their ongoing devotion to the narrative rendering of such stories, there is, I think, room for situating our teaching anew.

Works Cited

Kennedy, Liam. "Spectres of Comparison: American Studies and the United States of the West." *American Studies. An Anthology*. Ed. Janice A. Radway, Kevin K. Gaines, Barry Shank and Penny Von Eschen. Malden, MA: Wiley-Blackwell, 2009. 569-77.

Palumbo-Liu, David, ed. *The Ethnic Canon. Histories, Institutions, and Interventions*. Minneapolis: U Minnesota P, 1995.

Transoceanic Race
A Postcolonial Approach to Italian American Studies

Cristina Lombardi-Diop
Loyola University, Chicago

As a graduate scholar of African Studies, studying for the first time outside of Italy, I learned how the legacy of colonial culture had a significant impact not only on those nations—such as Britain and France—that had an uncontested imperial past, but also on my own country. Italy, after all, had created its own "minor empire" on the Red Sea, had given Eritrea its actual name, turned Libya into a "fourth shore," and claimed a protectorate over Somalia after it had lost its other colonies. The fact that I had discovered this significant and controversial part of Italian modern history not while residing in Italy but once I had become a migrant—a privileged one, for sure, but a migrant nonetheless—reveals the epistemological impact of both diasporic life and postcolonial historiography.

My dissertation work (Lombardi-Diop 1999) pivoted around one question: What did it mean to be Italian for the colonial settlers, women and men, who lived in the Italian colonies from 1890 onward, most of whom were of middle-class origin? (A history of the colonial peasant settlers is still to be written.) How did they perceive their class and racial privileges in relation to the Africans they had turned into colonial subjects? How had they expanded their sense of nationhood abroad, and how were class hierarchies, and regional and national affiliations, reconstructed in the colonial setting? My critical framework strived to apply to the Italian context what I had learned from Black Studies, Race Theory, and Postcolonial Studies. I soon realized that adapting a theoretical postcolonial framework to the study of Italian colonial history required a series of adjustments that would account for the specific history of diasporic movements, alongside the regional and class imbalances, that characterize the history of the Italians in the nineteenth and twentieth century. As one manifestation of Italy's 'many diasporas,'[1] the African colonies provided

[1] Reference here is to Donna Gabaccia's inspiring title. See Gabaccia.

From: *Transcending Borders, Bridging Gaps* (Calandra Institute, 2015)

the ground for the emergence of political and cultural models unique to the colonial context, yet also implicated in the larger framework of the transformations of *italianità* brought about by emigration and diasporic dispersion. Without undermining the import of conquest, racial privilege, and imperial claims inextricably embedded within the construction of colonizing subjectivities, it could be argued that the critical tools employed to analyze Italian colonial racial discourse may also shed light on the process of the formation of racial identity in other diasporic contexts, such as the building of Italian communities in the New World. Conversely, although rooted in the context of hegemonic white America, the study of Italian American racial models of *italianità* may illuminate aspects of colonial and postcolonial racial culture that might otherwise remain muted.

The emergence of new forms of racism in contemporary Italy and the analysis of race provide a fertile ground for probing the validity of connecting diverse diasporic contexts under the same theoretical umbrella and, more specifically, under the umbrella of postcolonial studies. As David Goldberg explains, "racial ideas, meanings, exclusionary and repressive practices in one place are influenced, shaped by, and fuel those elsewhere. Racial ideas and arrangements circulate, cross borders, shore up existing or prompt new ones as they move between established political institutions" (360). Let me go back to my own critical trajectory in order to explain my point. My interest in Italian colonial racial discourse had stemmed from the need, which I felt compelling at the time, to reconstruct a genealogy of the social perceptions and racist representations of African immigrants in Italy in the 1980s and 1990s, when racism had turned from being possible to being real,[2] and racializing processes were beginning to permeate the public sphere by cementing themselves around the idea of blackness as foreign and abject.

Returning to the colonial past as a point of departure seemed necessary, given the limitations intrinsic in a synchronic explanation of Italian racism as a contemporary phenomenon engendered exclusively by the demographic changes and the subsequent multiculturalism brought about by immigration. Such an explanation left the many transformations of racism over time unaccounted for, as it undermined the very idea that the as-

[2] I am referring here to the research, published in the early 1990s, on the emergent forms of racism by Laura Balbo e Luigi Manconi in *I razzismi possibili* (1990) and *I razzismi reali* (1992).

sumptions of race are always in process, always implicating multiple historical actors and stages. After all, racism is, fundamentally "a theory of history. It is a theory of who is who, who belongs and who does not, of who deserves what and who is capable of what. By looking at racial categories and their fluidity over time, we glimpse the competing theories of history which inform the society and define its internal struggles" (Jacobson 6). Multiculturalism itself, as a category of analysis, tends to conceal the specific historical links with the colonial racialist past. From the perspective of Italian migration and race studies, the postcolonial paradigm offers instead the possibility to add to the analysis of contemporary multicultural societies a diachronic dimension that moves the focus beyond the present, beyond the national context, and beyond the confines of one single disciplinary paradigm. Conversely, if we understand contemporary societies as postcolonial societies, postcoloniality can be refigured as a transnational and historical condition that affects not only contemporary Italians, but the very transformations of what it means to be Italian in a condition of diaspora.

What do we learn about the Italian diaspora and about race when we take a postcolonial approach to Italian American studies? The answer to this question is well illustrated in Robert Viscusi's article "The History of Italian American Literary Studies," where the critic and poet takes the epochal transformation of Italy from a country of emigration to a country of immigration as his starting point, in order to identify three major shifts in the history of Italian American literary studies: a colonial period (1820–1941), a postcolonial period (1941–1991), and a global one (1991–present). The single thread that connects these three periods is the position of cultural subalternity that Italian American culture has held both in relation to the metropolitan fatherland of origin during the 'colonial' period, and to the destination country during the 'postcolonial' period. Its effects were felt most of all at the level of language expression since, after all, both the Italian and the English language functioned as hegemonic national languages in relation to the regional dialects. Italian America as both a 'colony' of Italy and a 'colony' of the United States, experienced "two spatial hegemonies" (Viscusi 49), a situation that, I believe, aptly describes any diasporic postcolonial condition, in which the migratory movement becomes a movement from one colonial order to another. This condition of "double subalternity" is indeed a condition shared by many postcolonial writers in today's Italy, who have moved from forms of linguistic and cultural colonization in their countries of origin by their former European colonial powers, to a metropolitan center such as Italy where the hegemonic forms of *italianità* still run counter to a truly global and transcultural space of literary and cultural expression.

The identification of the multiple forms of Italian American subalternity also teaches us something important about the multiple trajectories of the Italian racial identity. In the Italian context, the study of racism has focused either on its historical forms or on contemporary institutional discrimination and individual racist practices, and has just lately begun to connect the two temporal periods.[3] Scholars have also looked at the European dimension of institutional forms of discrimination, showing an enhanced awareness of the global dynamics that link new capital mobility and labor production to immigration patterns and legal restrictions. Yet the social critique of racism has dedicated little attention to the ways in which race, as a system of differentiation, "shapes those on whom it bestows privilege as well as those it oppresses" (Frankenberg 519). To pay attention to race means to explore how modern Italian identity has been shaped by a series of racial perceptions and self-definitions that have structured and supported the idea of Italianness as racially coded.

In the field of Italian American studies, instead, the impetus to study Italian whiteness has advanced in considerable ways our understanding of racial identity within the Italian diasporic context. [4] Scholars have studied the place of Italian Americans along the U.S. color line, exploring what it means to be Italian in terms of race. Race, as a taboo term in Europe after the Holocaust and the racial violence of the imperial past, has returned to Italy and to Italian Studies through the analysis of the perception of Italian Americans as racially coded. Alongside the work by such historians and critics as David Roediger and Matthew Jacobson on ethnic whites, Italian American scholars have explored the kind of "fluidity of race" (Jacobson 8) that characterizes the process by which Italian Americans became white.

---

[3] I have discussed this point at greater length in previous work. For further bibliographical references see: Lombardi-Diop 2012a, and Giuliani and Lombardi-Diop.

[4] The seminal work in this direction was the volume edited by Jennifer Guglielmo and Salvatore Salerno, and the study of race relations for Italians in Chicago by Thomas Guglielmo, both published in 2003.

The history of the racialization of Italian Americans is instructive on many levels. Theories of race that had served to classify both the *meridionali* and the African colonial subjects in Italy travelled across the Atlantic in order to help creating a hierarchy of races among the new European immigrants on the American soil. Following the work of positivist anthropologists such as Alfredo Niceforo and Giuseppe Sergi, from 1899 onward the U.S. Bureau of Immigration and the US Immigration Commission began identifying two races for Northern and Southern Italians ("Keltic" for the former and "Iberian" for the latter), while social scientists and opinion makers began attributing civilized cultural traits to the Keltic race and semi-barbaric traits to the Iberian race, primitive also in virtue of their "Negroid ancestry" and deemed unfit to be full citizens of the United States (Thomas Guglielmo 34-35).[5] Italian Americans did not always benefited for being considered white, as their history began as one of lynching, discrimination, and segregation, a history they shared with other minorities in the United States. Anti-Italianism has been a pervasive experience of Italian immigration in the United States. In 1911, the Dillingham Commission published a *Dictionary of Races or People*, a taxonomic volume that enabled the Commission to create a hierarchy of colored races and place the new waves of immigration from Southern Europe in a category different from the Northern European ones, defined as "darker." The federal government instituted the practice of distinguishing between race and color, the former being a taxonomic category drawn from the positivist language of mid-nineteenth century raciology to distinguish among large transnational/ethnic groups (say, between the Celts and the Mediterraneans), the latter being a social category (Thomas Guglielmo 2003a, 8-9; Vellon 26-27) whose function was to serve various goals, but primarily the one to sustain a racial order based on the drawing of the color line between whites and nonwhites (Jacobson, chapter 2).

Naturalization laws in the United States had been burdened with racial restrictions since 1790; whiteness was 'naturally' linked to the privileges of citizenship up until 1870, when the 'white person' prerequisite was abolished for people of African descent, but persisted for other individuals, particularly Asians, until 1952 (Haney López 42-48; Jacobson 22-23). Naturalization procedures required applicants to specify both race and col-

[5] For a critique of Guglielmo's approach refer to Luconi 49-50.

or; "for Italians, the only acceptable answers were North or South Italian for the former and white for the latter" (Thomas Guglielmo 2003a, 9). If the status of Italians as Caucasians became a debatable and questionable issue, and if the Italians were discriminated and suffered prejudice and offences on the basis of racial prejudices, they were nonetheless never defined as a 'colored race' or as 'nonwhite' by the US immigration and the US census and, consequently, they were never denied naturalization rights on the basis of their color: "while Italians suffered for their supposed *racial* undesirability as Italians, South Italians, and so forth, they still benefited in countless ways from their privileged *color* status as white" (Thomas Guglielmo 2003, 33). Their whiteness had indeed something to do with their perceived cultural 'superiority' as the progeny of the earliest Greek civilization of Central and Southern Italy, considered as one of the birthplaces of Western civilization. "In the end, Italians' firm hold on whiteness never loosened over time [...] Italian Americans' whiteness—conferred more powerfully by the federal government than by any other institution—was their single most powerful asset in the 'New World'" (Thomas Guglielmo 2003, 41-43).

The history of the process of racialization (into whiteness, into blackness) of Italian Americans has been fraught with untold stories; recent literary and scholarly works have opened up the way to a critical examination of racial self-ascription and racism. In narrating the naturalization story of her grandmother, writer Louise DeSalvo observes that "The way my father (and mother, too) dealt with their Italian heritage was to not discuss it. Nor did they discuss *anyone*'s race, *anyone*'s ethnicity" (DeSalvo 18; emphasis in the original). In her brief memoir, race is a fractured line of identity, and it splits and recomposes—unresolved and lingering—the examination of the self in relation to family, neighborhood, community, and the American mainstream. Rosette Capotorto also painfully admits to her tortuous path to identity "along the race continuum": "I was raised to be a racist. Not the name-calling, dagger-carrying kind but the more subtle, insidious, 'some of my best friends,' let's uphold the neighborhood kind" where racism looms bigger than personal belief and social practices, a continuum where identity is not only determined by the individual free will but by the gaze of others ("when I walk past a 'gang,' meaning a 'group' of black teenage boys I feel the physical tension and I try to acknowledge it, render it real. [...] What do they see when they look at me?" (Capotorto and Painter 254). In her poem, "We begin with food," the term "black Italian" floats on the page with no signified attached; the poem is inserted within a chapter titled "Italiani/Africani," another floating signifier, where we read that "Sicilian is Black is African" (Capotorto and Painter 251). Similarly, Ronnie Mae Painter—musician, photographer, metal sculptor—born of a black father and a white mother, defines herself as "my Black self," and wonders "what makes me Italian?—finding the answer in a mixture of somatic and cultural traits ("What makes me Italian are my eyes and my mouth. If you look very closely at my eyes, you'll see Italy in them. From my mouth you will hear my mother, Beatrice. I say what I want, when I want, to whomever I want").[6]

The distinction between color/race presents itself as pivotal in the naturalization story by DeSalvo: "Becoming a naturalized citizen granted my grandmother (some) rights and privileges of a native-born American but neither the privilege of being completely accepted nor absorbed into the mainstream of North American life" (22). Naturalization—she reflects on the etymology of the term—is "*The action of making natural.* (Which, of course, means that what you were—Italian, in this case—was unnatural" (DeSalvo 23. Emphasis in the original.) The writer's grandmother was naturalized as 'white' in color but as 'dark' in complexion: "Dark made its implied meaning clear: my grandmother had become 'racialized'. To become a citizen, my grandmother had to perjure herself. She had to admit that she manifested an attribute that was not true, but that someone else had insisted was true" (28). Implicit in this statement is that the self-ascribed identity—which is understood as the truth of the 'natural' identity of the writer's grandmother as Italian—is indeed white, while the racialist attribution of darkness is false and imposed from above. Italian-ness and whiteness are thus 'naturally' reconciled in the writer's retrospective analysis; whiteness becomes the 'natural' attribute, erasing all possible awareness of its implicit privileges and the very possibility of its critique.

---

[6] Capotorto and Painter 252. Interestingly enough, the interrogation "What makes me Italian?" links this particular example of diasporic African Italian identity with other diasporic African Italian identities across the Atlantic and, in primis, the one voiced by Somali writer Igiaba Scego in her celebrated short-story "Salsicce." See Scego. In her salient reading of the intersection of blackness and Italian-ness in African Italian texts, Caterina Romeo connects Scego's work with other Italian American memoirs, including Kym Ragusa's. See Romeo.

DeSalvo's story reminds us that the association of Italianess with darkness lingers in the form of a traumatic memory passed down through generations; at the same time, the association of Italianess with whiteness creates a paradoxical invisibility: "Italian Americans are invisible people. Not because people refuse to see them, but because, for the most part, they refuse to be seen. Italian Americans became invisible the moment they could pass themselves off as being white. And since then they have gone to great extremes to avoid being identified as anything but white, they have even hidden the history of being people of color. [...] By becoming white, they have paid a price, and that price is the extinction of their culture" (Gardaphé 1). As Fred Gardaphé argues, one of the possible consequences of having made invisible the history of discrimination Italian Americans share with other groups in the United States is the loss of the power to discursively and visually represent themselves. I agree with Gardaphé that to bring this history to visibility is to read alternative versions of Italian American history, and a postcolonial lens enables us to do just that.

The instability of the racial identity of Italian Americans partakes of the larger, transnational history of Italian identity in the twentieth century. As David Roediger remarks, echoing W. E. B. Du Bois, the 1935 invasion of Ethiopia brought the history of Italy's racist prejudice to international attention, and that history highlights "the important connections of race, violence, diaspora, empire, and national feeling"; most importantly, the invasion provides a perspective on transoceanic race relations, as it reveals the historical continuum linking the racial identity of Italians in the United States with Italy's history of racism, prompting us to reflect "whether immigrants from Italy were ever white *before* arrival, or at least accustomed to race-thinking *before* arrival."[7] For the purpose of this essay, this is a very important connection to make, as it positions the history of race relations within a larger, transoceanic framework, where the ricocheting effects of colonial violence and imperial racism are understood beyond the confines of discreet national entities (Italy, the United States) and from the viewpoint of a postcolonial, transnational approach to Italy's racial history.

In conclusion, the critical and political implications inherent in fostering a postcolonial approach to Italian American studies are manifold:

---

[7] Roediger 2003, 261. Emphasis in the original. The reference here is to Thomas Guglielmo's pivotal study on Italian American race relations in Chicago. See Thomas Guglielmo 2003a.

- "Postcolonial" Italy is not simply a derivative of the more 'dominant' traditions of postcolonial studies, but adds a fresh and vital perspective on transoceanic and global postcolonialities;[8]
- Race relations are central to the historical formation of the Italian diasporic identity as they are to the contemporary Italian experience;
- An engaged postcolonial critique of such identity can engender the recovery of the historical memory of both colonialism and emigration;
- Italian-Americans critics, writers, and intellectuals have already foregrounded issues ("questions of recognition, visibility, and recovery"[9]) that are intrinsic to the postcolonial theoretical arena and that are shared by first and second-generation postcolonial writers in contemporary Italy;
- By emphasizing a comparative, transnational, and transoceanic critical exchange, a postcolonial approach to Italian diaspora studies represents a methodological disposition, an incitement to productively practice multidisciplinarity and finding new ways of doing and intersecting Italian and Italian American Studies.

I believe that our critical engagement should work in the direction of finding connections among the three phenomena of emigration, colonialism, and immigration[10] by encouraging further critical work that brings to light not only the history of racism but also the stories that tell us about who we are as Italians. This can be done by opening the historical archives, involving different institutional sites, and by telling and listening to our common—and often silenced—private stories.

---

[8] For a theorization of the paradigms that are foundational to Italian postcoloniality refer to the introductory chapter in Lombardi-Diop and Romeo 2012, 1-29, as well as to Lombardi-Diop and Romeo 2014.

[9] Giunta and Zamboni Mc Cormick 2.

[10] The efforts of the Italian American Studies Network, founded in Bellagio, go precisely in this direction.

WORKS CITED

Balbo Laura and Luigi Manconi. *I razzismi possibili*. Milan: Feltrinelli, 1990.

______. *I razzismi reali*. Milan: Feltrinelli, 1992.

Capotorto, Rosette. "My Mother is Black." Guglielmo and Salerno 254-256.

Connell, William J. and Fred Gardaphé, eds. *Anti-Italianism: Essays on a Prejudice*. New York: Palgrave Macmillan, 2010.

DeSalvo, Louise. "Color: White/Complexion: Dark." Guglielmo and Salerno 17-28.

Frankenberg, Ruth. "White Women, Race Matters." *Theories of Race and Racism: A Reader*. Ed. Les Back and John Solomos. London and New York: Routledge, 2006. 519-33.

Gabaccia, Donna R. *Italy's Many Diasporas*. New York and London: Routledge, 2003.

Gardaphé, Fred. "Invisible People. Shadows and Light in Italian American Culture." Connell and Gardaphé 1-22.

Giuliani, Gaia and Cristina Lombardi-Diop. *Bianco e nero. Storia dell'identità razziale degli italiani*. Florence: Le Monnier-Accademia, 2013.

Giunta, Edvige and Kathleen Zamboni McCormick, eds. *Teaching Italian American Literature, Film, and Popular Culture*. New York: The Modern Language Association of America, 2010.

Goldberg, Theo David. "The Comparative and the Relational: Meditations on Racial Method." *A Companion to Comparative Literature*. Ed. Ali Behdad and Dominic Thomas. Oxford, UK, Blackwell Publishing, 2011, 357-368.

Guglielmo, Jennifer, and Salvatore Salerno, eds. *Are Italians White? How Race is Made in America*. New York and London: Routledge, 2003.

Guglielmo, Thomas A. "'No Color Barrier': Italians, Race, and Power in the United States." Guglielmo and Salerno, 29-43, 2003.

______. *White on Arrival: Italians, Race, Color, and Power in Chicago, 1890-1945*. Oxford (UK): Oxford University Press, 2003a.

Haney López, Ian F. *White by Law: The Legal Construction of Race*. New York and London: New York University Press, 1996.

Jacobson, Matthiew Frye. *Whiteness of a Different Color: European Immigrants and the Alchemy of Race*. Cambridge, MA: Harvard University Press, 1999.

Lombardi-Diop, Cristina and Caterina Romeo, eds. *Postcolonial Italy: Challenging National Homogeneity*. New York: Palgrave Macmillan, 2012.

Lombardi-Diop, Cristina and Caterina Romeo. "The Italian Postcolonial: A Manifesto." *Italian Studies*, vol. 69 (November 2014): 425-33.

Lombardi-Diop, Cristina. "Postracial/Postcolonial Italy." Lombardi-Diop and Romeo, 2012. 175-90.

______. Writing the Female Frontier: Italian Women in Colonial Africa, 1890-1940. Ph.D. Thesis, New York University, 1999.

Luconi, Stefano. "L'identità etno-razziale degli italoamericani e il regime fascista." *Parlare di razza. La lingua del colore tra Italia e Stati Uniti*. Ed. Tatiana Petrovich Njegosh and Anna Scacchi. Rome: Ombre corte, 2012. 46-63.

Painter, Ronnie Mae, and Rosette Capotorto, *Italiani/Africani*. Guglielmo and Salerno, 250-58.

Roediger, David R. "Afterword. DuBois, Race, and Italian Americans." Guglielmo and Salerno, 259-263.

______. *Working Toward Whiteness: How America's Immigrants Became White. The Strange Journey from Ellis Island to the Suburbs*. New York: Basic Books, 2005.

Romeo, Caterina. "Racial Evaporations: Representing Blackness in African Italian Postcolonial Literature. Lombardi-Diop and Romeo, 2012, 221-236.

Scego, Igiaba. "Salsicce." *Pecore nere*. Ed. Flavia Capitani and Emanuele Coen. Bari: Laterza, 2005, 23-36.

Vellon, Peter. "'Between White Men and Negroes': The Perception of Southern Italian Immigrants through the Lens of Italian Lynching." Connell and Gardaphé, 23-32.

Viscusi, Robert. "The History of Italian American Literary Studies." Giunta and Zamboni McCormick, 43-58.

Remapping the Field
A Transnational/International American Studies Perspective on Italian/American Studies

Giorgio Mariani
"Sapienza" University of Rome

Like other "turns" in literary and cultural studies—from the linguistic turn of a few decades ago to the more recent cognitive one—also what has been variously dubbed as the "international," the "cosmopolitan," the "global", the "post-national," or "transantional" turn in American studies has been the object of heated critical debates concerning its origins, its nature, and its scopes. One could begin by noticing that all the adjectives just highlighted in quotation marks, while implicitly referring to the crisis of nation-based paradigms and epistemologies, mean rather different things to different people. Though practitioners of the approaches associated with these adjectives all share a desire to situate "America" within a much expanded—both temporally and spatially—historical, political, social, and cultural context, they often disagree not only on what may be the most effective ways to do so but also on their overt or covert ideological implications. This is obviously not the place to attempt a thorough mapping of a continuously evolving field of study. All I wish to do here is sketch some of the coordinates of what, for the sake of brevity, I shall call TAS/IAS (Transnational American Studies / International American Studies), knowing full well that while these terms are sometimes used interchangeably, to many they designate different kinds of comparative work. More generally, however, my aim is to suggest how TAS/IAS may intersect the field of Italian/American studies and help us to reimagine it as part of a larger American/Italian discourse beyond the geographical contours of the U.S. One of the main advantages of such reconfiguration, I shall argue, is that of forestalling the appropriation of the Italian/American narrative by what Amy Kaplan has called "the tenacious grip of American exceptionalism," which remain strong even in the age of multiculturalism.[1]

[1] On the emergence of multiculturalism "as a quintessential American value, marking the United States as a unique society among nations" see Sanchez.

From: *Transcending Borders, Bridging Gaps* (Calandra Institute, 2015)

All shorthand definitions of TAS/IAS are open to criticism. Take, for example, the founding declaration of the International American Studies Association (IASA), created in Bellagio, on June 1, 2000, largely thanks to the efforts of Djelal Kadir. As one can read on the association's website, "The International American Studies Association (IASA) was founded today by twenty-two scholars from around the world, committed to the study of America—regionally, hemispherically, nationally, and transnationally. Rooted in various fields of study, the IASA will provide a space for interdisciplinary dialogues about American culture and society. To this purpose, it will promote international exchanges of teachers, scholars, and students and generate debates, publications, and conferences" (Bellagio). One could easily object that this statement says both too much and too little. For starters, some may take issue with its implicit use of terms like "international" and "transnational" as synonyms. Others may point to the fact that this founding statement, perhaps deliberately, does not clarify whether "America" is largely another term for the US, or whether it refers to the whole continent.[2] Some may also lament that, from such a brief statement, it is not easy to grasp in what ways the "international exchanges" the IASA wished to sponsor would be different from the more traditional ones promoted under the aegis of the U.S. State Department since the end of the Second World War. Finally, there is no explicit mention here of that desire to "de-center" an older American Studies by moving beyond a nation-based ontology towards a global or planetary perspective that many would associate with the notion of a "transnational" or "international" turn in American Studies.

At this point one may get the impression that my aim is to launch a critique of the founding moment of the association I currently have the honor of presiding. However, that is by no means my goal. My point is simply to call attention to the fact that all definitions of TAS/IAS are at risk of appearing either too vague or too limiting. For example, this is how John Carlos Rowe defines TAS in an entry for *the Encyclopedia of American Studies*. "The 'transnational turn' in American studies refers generally to

[2] It is only fair to add, however, that one of the first Association's Articles specifies that its goal is "to further the international exchange of ideas and information among scholars from all nations and various disciplines who study and teach America regionally, hemispherically, nationally, and transnationally." Moreover, the IASA World Congresses have always welcomed not only workshops on hemispheric studies and on countries other than the U.S. but also presentations in all the major languages of the Americas.

scholarship in the past twenty years that has stressed the comparative study of the different 'Americas'—Latin America, the Caribbean, the United States—and Canada as the appropriate objects of study for the discipline. 'Transnationalism' also refers to American studies done by international scholars outside the United States, especially scholarship that emphasizes the influence of the United States abroad." This, I think, is a pretty good and incisive description, and I agree with most of the ideas it conveys. The idea, for example, that TAS is not concerned exclusively with the U.S., but aims at developing a hemispheric perspective. I also think that the adjective "comparative" is a crucial one. Whatever else TAS might be, it is a field of study (though some may prefer to call it a methodological approach) in which different national, sub-national, or regional entities are brought to bear on one another in ways that allow for hitherto hidden dimensions of texts and contexts to emerge. At the same time, however, I am somewhat troubled by the timeframe Rowe adopts. He is correct, I think, in dating the transnational turn to the post-1989 moment, when the launching of globalization, with its concurrent notion of the weakening of national states and national identities, called for new paradigms and new models across a vast array of disciplines, the humanities in all their ramifications included. Besides the founding of the IASA, there are at least three key items often quoted as presiding over the birth of TSA / IAS. The La Pietra Conferences, organized by Thomas Bender since 1997, which resulted eventually in the publication of the 2002 anthology *Rethinking American History in a Global Age*, calling for a study of U.S. history that would take into account its manifold connections to the rest of the world. Robert Gross's article "The Transnational Turn: Rediscovering American Studies in a Wider World," appearing in the December 2000 issue of the *Journal of American Studies*, where, perhaps for the first time, it was openly stated that "To globalize American Studies is to displace American perspectives on the subject" (384). Shelley Fisher Fiskin answered to, and expanded on, this call to decenter older paradigms in an often-cited presidential address, delivered at the American Studies Association meeting in 2004. Later published in *American Quarterly*, Fisher Fiskin's address stated, among other things, that "The goal of American studies scholarship is not exporting and championing an arrogant, pro-American nationalism but understanding the multiple meanings of America and American culture in all their complexity" (20).

So there is no question that only over the last twenty or so years we have begun to pay closer attention to the fact that no culture, no literature, no economy, no social formation can be studied and understood within an isolated geographical/historical/political space, usually that of the nation. However, if—as John Rowe claims—scholarship on the U.S. by non-U.S. scholars is seen as one of the other main features of TAS/IAS, then it seems odd to contain the latter into such an incredibly short time-span. The U.S.—as well as, of course, the other nations that comprise the American continent—has been studied and written about by non-U.S. scholars for centuries, not a few decades. What should we do with these works? Are they part of the TAS/IAS archive, or are they something else, because they seemed to be informed by different theoretical preoccupations? Here I realize I am essentially repeating a point I already made some years ago, when I contributed a short piece to a discussion of "transatlanticism". There I wrote that, "Even though they may not have used the term 'transatlanticism,' there is no question that Americanists operating outside the US have always been aware of the comparative dimension of their intellectual work. To stick to my field of specialization, European students of the literatures of the Americas have traditionally devoted considerable attention to both the ways in which American texts were received in various European countries and to the reception of European texts in the Americas. The question is, should we consider, say, studies of Italian or German reception of Emerson's work, or of Emerson's use of Dante and Goethe, transatlantic or not?" (Mariani 7). What I said about "transatlantic" studies, I believe applies as well to "transnational" or "international" American Studies. Does all comparative work fall under these umbrella terms, or should we expect TAS/IAS to be guided by specific theoretical and political preoccupations?

Of course, one might well ask whether it really matters what label we attach to the comparative work people do. For example, to speak again of something I have written about, is the study of the influence of Emerson's and Thoreau's ideas about non-violence on Gandhi, and in turn the influence of Gandhi's thought circling back to the U.S. to shape Martin Luther King's own thinking, an example of transnational or international American Studies? My impression is that both labels could apply, at least as I understand them. Civil disobedience certainly did not spring piecemeal from Thoreau's mind the way Athena emerged from Jove's head. It has roots in Christian—that is Middle-Eastern—thought as much as in Far Eastern philosophy, but it also draws on key Enlightenment principles. In brief, one could easily argue that civil disobedience is part of an ideoscape—to use Arjun Appadurai's term—with no precise point of origin, an example of an ante-litteram global cultural flow. On the other hand, no serious analysis of how non-violence was operative in 1930s and 40s India, or during the Civil Rights era in the U.S., can be even attempted without taking into account the power struggles between specific nation-states. As Mary Dudziak has shown, for example, the Civil Rights movement can be properly understood only once it is seen within the context of the Cold War. While both TAS and IAS are explicitly and inevitably comparative in nature, my understanding is that the former tend to focus more on what Zygmunt Bauman identifies as the liquid aspect of modernity, while the latter are wary of too hastily liquidating the nation-state as both a political and an analytic unit. From my perspective, therefore, TAS and IAS may well privilege different kinds of approaches but need not be incompatible.

What significance, if any, may this whole debate have in respect to the development of Italian-American studies within the larger framework of American Studies? The emphasis that TAS place on cultural flows and hybridization could encourage scholars of Italian/American studies to venture beyond their traditional domains. They would of course continue to investigate the cultural work done by people of Italian descent within the US, and the ways in which Italian Americans and Italy are portrayed in US literature, media, political discourse, etc., but they might also be drawn to areas so far left relatively unexplored. For example, a great deal has been written on the literary and cinematic representation of the Mafia, a topic of paramount importance for a host of obvious reasons. It seems to me, however, that as far as cinema goes, more attention could be paid to a genre like the so-called "Spaghetti Western" and its tradition, which should not be studied only by scholars with an interest in the Western, but by anyone who is curious about the cultural relations between the U.S. and Italy. The cultural flows of the Western ideoscape are incredibly rich and complex, with Sergio Leone and others learning from the U.S., and then becoming teachers in their own right, playing no small role in the creation of what is usually considered a quintessential American icon like Clint Eastwood. More recently, the Italian American Quentin Tarantino has tapped again into the archive of the Italian Western for his important and

As in Roland Barthes' seminal *S/Z*, the slash should have the function of calling attention to the material—linguistic, cultural, and ideological—processes through which the very terms "Italian" and "American" are constituted. The slash between Italian and American should function to evoke that "third," "neither/nor" space that abolishes the antithesis between the two terms and challenges the identity of each by disturbing the positionality upon which their representativeness lies.

WORKS CITED

Appadurai, Arjun. *Modernity at Large. Cultural Dimensions in Globalization.* Minneapolis: Minnesota UP, 1996.

Bauman, Zygmunt. *Liquid Modernity.* Cambridge: Polity Press, 2012.

Barthes, Roland. *S/Z.* London: Jonathan Cape, 1974.

Bellagio, June 1, 2000. http://iasaweb.org/about/history.html. Web.

Bender, Thomas, ed. *Rethinking American History in a Global Age.* Berkeley and Los Angeles: U of California P, 2002.

Berthold, Dennis. *American Risorgimento.* Columbus: Ohio State UP, 2009.

Dudziak, Mary. *Cold War Civil Rights: Race and the Image of American Democracy.* Princeton: Princeton UP, 2000.

Edwards, Brian T. and Dilip Parameshwar Gaonkar. "Introduction." *Globalizing American Studies.* Chicago: U of Chicago P, 2010. 1-44.

Fiskin, Shelley Fisher. "Crossroads of Cultures: The Transnational Turn in American Studies – Presidential Address to the American Studies Association, November 12, 2004." *American Quarterly* 57.1 (2005): 17-57.

Gross, Robert. "The Transnational Turn: Rediscovering American Studies in a Wider World." *Journal of American Studies* 34.3 (2000). 373–93.

Kaplan, Amy. "The Tenacious Grip of American Exceptionalism." *Comparative American Studies: An International Journal* 2.2 (2004): 153-59.

Mariani, Giorgio. "Transatlanticism Then and Now?" *Review of International American Studies* 1.1 (2006): 7-9. http://iasaweb.org/publications/rias.html. Web.

Rowe, John Carlos. "Transnationalism and American Studies." *Encyclopedia of American Studies.* Ed. Simon J. Bronner. Baltimore: Johns Hopkins University Press, 2014. http://eas-ref.press.jhu.edu/view?aid=794. Web.

Sanchez, George J. "Creating the Multicultural Nation: Adventures in Post-Nationalist American Studies in the 1990s." *Post-Nationalist American Studies.* Ed. John Carlos Rowe. Berkeley and Los Angeles: U of California P, 2000. 40-62.

Tamburri, Anthony, *To Hyphenate or Not to Hyphenate. The Italian/American Writer: An* Other *American.* Montreal: Guernica, 1991.

Tarantino, Quentin. "Far West Tarantino." *Il Manifesto.* Sept. 25, 2010. 16

The Development of Italian-American Studies and the Italian Diaspora Altreitalie Center Activities

Maddalena Tirabassi
Centro Altreitalie-Globus et Locus

Research on the history of Italian migration resumed with vigor in the early eighties, in the wake of the "discovery" of the importance of the ethnic dimension in the countries of the great migration destination, particularly in the United States. Until then there had been a sort of division of labor between those who dealt in Italian emigration who looked mainly to the economic aspect and the impact of the phenomenon on the country and who, abroad, devoted to the study of the social integration of immigrants. In the early eighties the Giovanni Agnelli Foundation began a series of research programs to bridge this break by putting in contact Italian and foreign scholars.

The initiative resulted in the publication in 1987 of *Euroamerican,* three volumes dedicated to the people of Italian origin in the United States, Argentina and Brazil[1]. *Euroamerican* in fact includes contributions of Italian and foreign historians and sociologists that trace the history and methods of settlement of the people of Italian descent in the Americas. The project started from the finding of a lack of knowledge in Italy of the studies that were undertaken overseas on Italian migrations. In this sense, *Euroamericani* represented the first attempt to bridge the gap between Italian and American scholars

The Center

The Altreitalie Center was founded in 2005 under the auspice of the Giovanni Agnelli Foundation, and since 2009 is part of the Association Globus et Locus whose president is Piero Bassetti and carries out its projects with the support of the San Paolo Company under the direction of Maddalena Tirabassi, together with a Scientific Commit-

[1] Aa. Vv., *Euroamerican, La popolazione di origine italiana negli Stati Uniti, in Argentina, in Brasile*, 3 voll. (Torino, Edizioni F.G.A., 1987).

From: *Transcending Borders, Bridging Gaps* (Calandra Institute, 2015)

tee. The Center promotes itself as a body committed to the study of the Italian migrations in the world, following their geographical and historical evolution. Its success is due in part to a constant program of research and update, made available through the journal *Altreitalie. International Journal of Studies on Italian Migrations in the World*, the website, in Italian (www.altreitalie.it) and in English (www.altreitalie.org), Facebook, LinkedIn. The library has an ample and updated selection of volumes, rare books, journals, magazines and newsletter, and a small photo collection. It is open daily to the public. Other initiatives in the past have included the Altreitalie Academy, held for the training and updating of young scholars, Italian and foreign, interested in the study of migrations; a prize for the best Italian and foreign theses; research scholarships and grants.

ALTREITALIE

The first issue of the journal was delivered in 1989 and it's on online since 1996. Articles are published in the original language of the authors. It has an international scientific committee.[2]

Altreitalie was started to create a forum for scholars from every country and various disciplines on the issue of Italian migratory phenomenon and Italian communities. We immediately took advantage of the Internet opportunity: in 1996 we created a website and put *Altreitalie* on line. It was the first Italian journal to appear in full text and free on the web. The web helped the development of the transnational scholarship on migrations. It started to bridge the gap between scholars of the country of emigration and those in the countries of settle-

[2] Members: Patrizia Audenino, Università degli Studi di Milano; Paola Corti, Università di Torino; Francesco Durante, Università di Napoli "Suor Orsola Benincasa"; Emilio Franzina, Università di Verona; Claudio Gorlier, Università di Torino; Anna Maria Martellone, Università di Firenze; Chiara Vangelista, Università di Genova; Gianfranco Cresciani, Historical Consultant, Australia, New South Wales Australia; Luis de Boni, Universidade Federal do Rio Grande do Sul; Fred Gardaphè, Stony Brook University; Pasquale Petrone, Universidade de São Paulo; Bruno Ramirez, Université de Montréal; Lydio e Silvano Tomasi, Center for Migration Studies, New York. Among the founding fathers: Marcello Pacini, its first Director, George Pozzetta, Rudolph Vecoli, Raffaele Cocchi, Gianfausto Rosoli, Rovilio Costa, Luigi Favero, Ira Glazier, and Luigi De Rosa.

ment breaking a long-standing tradition which sow history of emigration and history of settlement as two separate fields of investigation.

The Data Banks

The data banks on passengers lists, created in 1993 and put on line in 2000 offer three on line data banks of the project "Find Your Roots" with the transcription of the information contained in the passenger lists of the ships that arrived in New York (1880-1891), Buenos Aires (1882-1920) and Vitoria (1858-1899). In the beginning they were the main attraction

The use people made of our passengers' list tell us much about identity. We noticed an increase of visitors to our website from Argentina (where the roots rush had not started yet) and Brazil. The website and the lists were used to obtain information to get Italian citizenship papers in order to leave the country.

Museums and Virtual Museums

The Altreitalie Center has been involved in the debate on the issue of the development of the public history of Italian migrations.[3] For decades Italian migrations have been considered a family matter in that people talked about migrations among relatives and friends. In Italy emigration has never been considered part of the nation building process despite the fact that it has been the protagonist of the biggest migration in the modern era, to quote Ferdinand Braudel, with 29

---

3 Maddalena Tirabassi, "Musei reali e virtuali," in Norberto Lombardi e Lorenzo Principe (a cura di), *Museo nazionale delle migrazioni. L'Italia nel mondo. Il mondo i Italia* (Rome: Ministero degli Affari Esteri, 2008) 159-63; Id., "Musei virtuali e reali sulle migrazioni," in *Studi Emigrazione*, 167 (2008): 754-61; Id., *I luoghi della memoria delle migrazioni*, in Paola Corti e Matteo Sanfilippo, *Annali* (Turin: Einaudi, 2009) 709-23; Id., "Migrazioni e segni italiani nel mondo," *TAO*, Torino, OAT, 4 (2010): 30-33; Id., Video "Segni italiani," OAT, Torino (2010); "Musei e migrazioni," *La Nuova Museologia* (2010): 9-13; Id., "How the ICT has changed the agenda of Italian migration studies and affected Italian migrants descendants' identities," *AEMI Journal*, 9 (2011): 30-35; Id., "Le migrazioni nelle iniziative per i 150 anni dell'unità d'Italia," *Rapporto Italiani nel mondo 2012* (Rome: Fondazione Caritas Migrantes) 133-40; Id., "La storia pubblica delle migrazioni italiane: mostre, musei, centri di ricerca e riviste," in Casmirri, Silvana, eds, *L'emigrazione italiana in 150 anni di storia unitaria*, Atti del convegno, 13-14 ottobre 2011 (Cassino: Università degli Studi di Cassino e del Lazio Meridionale, 2013) 63-77.

million people leaving the country between 1860 and 2010. In the post WWII decades, while internal and international migrations still affected millions of persons who went in northern Italy, Europe and in Latin American countries, the discourse on migration was still a very "private" one. Only recently Italians have started to consider their migratory experience not as a personal experience, but as a national one thanks to several factors:

- 1973 marks the point in which Italy, a country of emigration, turned into a country of immigration (the numbers of immigrants overcome that of emigrants), an event that initiated a debate on migration issues;
- Regioni, Italian regional district, established in the late sixties, started to pay attention to the communities created abroad by their former migrants;
- The political debate on the voting rights of Italians abroad focused Italian public attention on the outcomes of a century of migrations.
- Furthermore, in the 1980s, old emigrants, or their descendants, started to apply for documents to re-enter their country of origin from Latin America, Argentina and Brazil, affected by the economic crisis;
- The ICT also played an important role, facilitating contacts between former migrants and the country of origin, strengthening the relationship and reinforcing cultural ties.

One of the first sign of the "discovery" of Italian migrations was given by the increase in the number of exhibitions. From a small database on exhibitions that we started building in the portal Altreitalie (www.altreitalie.it; Exhibitions and Museums section) can be counted, since 1980, forty. Mainly they have been set locally by public or private entities, with two exceptions: Italy outside Italy—Pictures of Immigration (by Maria Rosaria Ostuni and Paola Agosti), held at the "Second national Conference of migration," Rome, 28 November to 3 December 1988 and Tantepatrieunapatria, (by the Foundation Paolo Cresci and CSER January–March 15, 2003) presented at the Vittoriano in Rome, supported by the Ministry of Italians in the World.

The same pattern was followed by museums: we have many migration museums, approximately thirty; most of them focus on a local or regional migratory experience.

Local museums appear to be important in making people gather out of attics and cellars memories, photographs, letters to be shown in the museum. A museum on migrations has a double effect: it makes common people experiences part of history and helps to collect materials. Some local museums are fuelled also by materials of the descendants of migrants who visit the birthplace of their ancestors during the summer.

The year 2011 has been important to Italian history because it was celebrated the 150 anniversary of the foundation of the Italian State. The challenge for us scholars of migration was to fully include migrants and their history into the public debate of Italian identity. The exhibition *Fare gli italiani* (*Making Italians*), the largest exhibition ever made on Italian history, included a section on migration as one to the main themes of the history of the country to show that almost all Italians have had a migratory.

THE NATIONAL MUSEUM OF ITALIAN EMIGRATION, MEI

Like Argentina and France, which have belatedly recognized the contribution of migration to the formation of their countries, Italy, in recent years, has started to recognize the long history of Italian migration as a cornerstone of the past and present of the nation.

The National Museum of Italian Emigration in the Vittoriano complex in Rome was created starting from these considerations: to network the many museums and research centers at the local or national level that have been dealing with decades of Italian migrations. The Museo dell'Emigrazione Italiana is located in Rome in a highly symbolic location that helps remedy the neglect of the country's history of migration. The MEI collects materials from local museums and existing centers, as well as private collections. The word emigration is not random, the collections are in fact dedicated to reconstruct the historical phases of migration from the unification of Italy to this day, and it lacks a discourse on recent immigration, except for a section at the end.

The paradigm of the Italian migration figures, duration, variety of destinations and origins is a complex phenomenon that includes the internal migration, with over 4 million registered in the AIRE and 60 million descendants in the world. Migration not only characterize the history of the Italian state, but the Italian peninsula since ancient times. Italy has participated with its population movements to the first and second globalization, a reality that has seen and sees men and women from different origins migrate in various contexts. But Italian migratory experience and the huge research done on it had not helped much either to elaborate the policies of integration (of the new immigrants) nor to fight discrimination. The reason was just in the lack of public recognition of the figure of the emigrant (historically considered a second class citizen) and his removal from the history of the country.

The aim was thus to inform and to account for the complexity of a phenomenon that is one of the great challenges of our time. A phenomenon of this magnitude could not touch the same sense of Italian identity in the economic, social, cultural and political as any time in the history of the peninsula was characterized by migration. Presenting the story of Italian sometimes the victims of xenophobia and racism, but also protagonists of successful integration as an integral part of Italian history and identity can help to address the issues raised by contemporary migration. Until Italians don't recognize that migrations are part of the history and identity of Italy, we will not be able to adequately address the issues raised by contemporary migrations.

Research

The Altreitalie Center has carried on various research projects on emerging themes.

I motori della Memoria. In 2007, under request of a group of Argentine women of Piedmont's origins belonging to an ethnic organization, the Foro delle donne piemontesi d'Argentina—an umbrella organization that gathered tens of association—the Region Piedmont asked Altreitalie Center to organize a research on the history of the Italian women in the country. The request was prompted by a desire of Argentine women of Piedmontese descent to understand their ethnic cultural identity, but also to replenish a vacuum in historiography, since the history of immigrant women in Argentina is one of the many stories that has not yet been written.[4] The construction of regional identities among Italian migrants is relatively recent: it is due to the constitution of the Regioni in Italy at the beginning of the 1970s. Up till then migrants had eventually kept personal contacts with the small village of origin. The Regione Piemonte has been particularly active in building up numerous programs dedicated to its citizens or their descendants abroad

In order to develop our research, we built up a semi-structured questionnaire, based on 30 questions, which was put online and was accessible through the website. The web made our research possible since, even though Italian migrants in Argentina are concentrated in specific areas, we can find them in the most remote sites of the big country.

Thanks to the engagement of the Foro, other Piedmontese associations and volunteers, who advertised and promoted the survey via web through the whole country, we were able to obtain 1,176 contacts. 835 questionnaires were sorted out as completed and used for the statistical work. The second part of the inquiry consisted in collecting tens of in depth interviews, to have qualitative material to interpret the questionnaire.

Italian/Piedmontese identity in some cases came out with the political and economic crisis in Argentina as in other Latin American countries such as Brazil. At the end of the seventies and the beginning of the eighties, in the course of seven years of dictatorship at least 30,000 people disappeared, of whom 200 were Italian citizens and approximately 10,000 of Piedmontese origins. The dictatorship forced many young people to leave Argentina in the attempt to escape from prison torture and murder. In this occasion many Argentines seemed to remember their not so distant European origins. The Italian passport was seen as a gateway to the European Union and therefore used as a kind of Visa to the European countries, which offered the best conditions concerning employment and language facilities. The consequence was a growth of 300% of Italian residents in Spain of whom roughly 60% came from Argentina. This erroneously called "return

[4] The results of the research have been published in Tirabassi, 2010.

migration" had very little to do with the traditionally called cultural identity. It was rather a glocal identity at work.

Those who choose Italy had the chance to get in touch with the ancestors' culture. In this case the "flight" to Italy was strongly connected to the discovery of the Italian language and the culture.

Our survey shows that very few did emigrate. Confirming the results of our previous research on Italian citizenship, the big majority went to Spain (more than 70%) while 24% migrated to other European countries. Most of them moved alone (65%) pushed by economical motivations (78%), or social and familiar reasons (respectively 21% and 13%). Research done on Italian descendants in Brazil show that the first country of emigration of Italobrazilians is the United States.

La meglio Italia. Our most recent research, started in 2012 and now published in a book *La meglio Italia. Le nuove mobilità nel XXI secolo* (Torino, Accademia UP, 2014), is dedicated to the new Italian migrations. We made a questionnaire and put it on line for three months. The findings have be integrated with in depth interviews, and the analysis of the census data of the many countries of immigration in order to quantify the new migrations since, with European open boarders, it has became very hard to know the exact figures.

The book writes the last chapter of Italian migration history that has numbers of five digit zeros: 106,000 in 2012, an increase of 115% compared to 2002 and an increase between 2011 and 2012 of 28.8% (Istat, 2013). 100,000 units had been touched for the first time at the beginning of the great emigration in 1880! It is difficult to quantify emigration since the migrants today cross European borders without visas and residence permits and often do not cancel registry from the last place of residence in Italy. As a result, the actual size of the phenomenon far exceeds the official figures and, according to some estimates, it can more than double. To give some examples, in the UK alone over the period March 2012–March 2013, there were 32,800 requests of the tax code / health card by Italians. In Spain, in 2012, 12,013 were registered in Spanish statistical office (INE), while the Department of Immigration in Australia for 2013 indicates the presence of 18,610 Italian citizens with short-term visas.

To leave Italy are not only skilled workers, or the brain drain ("cervelli in fuga"), but also students, professionals, technicians, entrepreneurs, researchers, retirees, volunteers and other personnel, qualified or not, who come from every region. Compared with the migrations of the past, however, the motivations change: the research shows that work is not always the main reason to leave the country, people also emigrate to seekin search of a better quality of life, for love, or to study.

La meglio Italia is the first attempt to write a history of contemporary Italian migrations: it confronts Italian statistical data with those of the main countries of immigration and it presents the results of an online questionnaire and in-depth interviews. This has allowed us to analyze in-depth the causes that push Italian citizens to leave the country, starting from the situation of young people, the first victims of unemployment.

The direct testimony of 1,500 Italians abroad and over 50 in-depth interviews paint a portrait of the migrants of globalization, of the "glo-migrants," as we started to call them since we still do not have a definition for the protagonists of the new phenomenon. As for work, there is a general improvement in the conditions of contract, but salaries vary greatly depending on the training, the country of settlement, and also depend on individual choices. Emerge also the difficulties and sacrifices in the new contexts: long working hours, both in universities and in the pizzerias, sometimes insufficient wages, job insecurity and difficulties due to extremely harsh weather and environmental conditions. A positive note is given by the levels of integration that are good in terms of social and cultural life. We have the emergence of a generation of Italians no longer provincial, if not cosmopolitan. Compared to the past there are several traits that diversify the old and new migration: the new migration is predominantly educated, with high language skills, is composed by individual, and the female component almost equals that of men. Never appears, among the reasons that lead to the decision to leave Italy, to send money home, the word remittance does not pertain to this migration.

Only half of the respondents are enrolled to the AIRE, Registry of Italians living abroad. One reason is because migration today is more mobile since one can easily live three months in a country and then decide to go to another while bureaucracy is very slow in changing one's residence. Also many of them do not want to cancel their Italian residence in order to get a new one because of the strong ties they still have with their hometown. Contemporary Italian migrants are bearers of transnational—regional and/or local—identities that show the necessity of a reinterpretation or readjusting of the old national parameters on citizenship rights. Census data, AIRE registration, the right to vote are just few of the issue to be addressed to meet the needs of a new mobile population.

Migrants of globalization are moving by choice, or at least they are almost all convinced of this. There remains, however, the risk that youth unemployment, and difficulties in finding a job, become the first strong motivation to emigrate turning a phenomenon characterized by the reversibility of choice and the transitional character, due to the dynamics of globalization, into a real escape of the "best Italian."

Altreitalie and Italian-American Studies

The involvement of Altreitalie in Italian-American issues dates back to the Agnelli Foundation programs in the eighties when research, grants, translations, hosting of visiting scholars and publications started.[5] U.S. scholars have always been on the journal board, as book review editors, Teresa Fiore, Evelyn Ferraro, Kenyon Zimmer. In every issue we review Italian-American books. Various essays have been published on Italian-American history, literature, sociology, film, etc.[6]

---

[5] For a list of the publications on Italian emigration to the U.S. see the website www.altreitalie.it. The first was Marcello Pacini (ed.), *Euroamericani, La popolazione di origine italiana negli Stati Uniti,* 1 (Turin: Fondazione Giovanni Agnelli, 1987).

[6] Paola Melone, "Arte e intercultura: l'Italian-American Visual Artists' Network (Iavanet)," *Altreitalie,* 44 (2012): 75-85; Tommaso Caiazza, "Pratiche e limiti della penetrazione fascista nelle comunità italoamericane: il caso della Scuola Italiana di San Francisco," *Altreitalie,* 45 (2012): 41-72; Giuseppe Calderone, "Il progetto delle colonie agricole negli Stati Uniti della grande emigrazione," *Altreitalie,* 46 (2013): 31-56; Teresa Fava Thomas, "Arresting the Padroni Problem in America 1881-1901: Italian Diplomats, Immigration Restrictionists, and the Italian Bureau," *Altreitalie*, 40 (2010): 57-81; Michele Presutto, "L'uomo che fece esplodere Wall Street. La storia di Mario Buda," *Altreitalie*, 40 (2010): 83-109; Stefano Luconi, "From William C. Celentano to Barack Obama: Ethnic and Racial Identity in Italian-American Postwar Political Experience, 1945-2008," *Altreitalie,* 38-39 (2009): 7-22; Susanna Scarparo, "Italian Proxy Brides in Australia," *Altreitalie*, 38-39 (2009): 85-108; Silvia Cassamagnaghi "Relax Girls, U.S. Will Treat You Right Le spose italiane dei GI della Seconda guerra mondiale," *Altreitalie*, 38-39 (2009): 109-

In a way, the Agnelli Foundation, first, and the Altreitalie Center, Globus et Locus, more recently, have contributed to fill a gap created in the Italian Universities on the teaching of Italian-American history and emigration in general. Today, while migration history is taught widely, Italian-American history, due to various reasons: a diminishing of academic positions in American history, new emerging field in migration studies, seems to me to be still little explored, but in the field of American studies, but also in this case stress is put on literature more than on history.

34; Mirco Melanco, "Appunti di viaggio dell'emigrato italiano nel cinema," *Altreitalie*, 38-39 (2009): 253-89; Silvana Tuccio, "Giorgio Mangiamele's The Spag," *Altreitalie*, 38-39 (2009): 289-300; Fred Gardaphè, "Le ombre e la luce: la rinascita della cultura italoamericana attraverso i film di gangster," *Altreitalie*, 38-39 (2009): 301-13; John Calabro, "The Children of Immigrants; Who Speaks for Them?," *Altreitalie*, 38-39 (2009): 315-24; Katia Ballacchino, "Il Giglio di Nola a New York. Uno sguardo etnografico sulla festa e i suoi protagonisti," *Altreitalie*, 36-37 (2008): 275-89; Gianfranco Zucca e Danilo Catania, "Dove il grattacielo incontra il cielo. Tempo biografico e commemorazione storica nei giovani di origine italiana di New York e San Francisco," *Altreitalie*, 36-37 (2008): 290-300; Matteo Pretelli, "Il Fascismo e gli italoamericani di seconda generazione," *Altreitalie*, 36-37 (2008): 301-13; Sebastiano Marco Cicciò, "L'etnicità va in guerra: l'impatto della Seconda guerra mondiale sulla comunità italoamericana," *Altreitalie*, 36-37 (2008): 314-23.

Perspectives on Critique and Italian American Studies[1]

Peter Carravetta
Stony Brook University

> ...there is no telling who does not own a
> stone in the Great Wall of China
>
> —*Herman Melville*

The comments that follow are predicated on an idea of interpretation, still in embryonic form, which can be called topological critique. Of course, I don't mean topological in the sense of the mathematical subdiscipline of topology, but, rather, in terms of a rehabilitation of a critique of the *topos*, the common-place, the site of occurrence of an exchange, in the tradition of Protagoras, Aristotle, Cicero, Quintilian, Vico, and Perelman. Background to this proposal is the notion that critique requires a theory, a method, and a rhetoric or form of discourse that conjoins and enables the two in order to properly frame and subsequently interpret a given social or cultural phenomenon. Critique requires a consciousness, a positing that instantly situates the speaker/writer within a context or community and which moreover establishes his/her political perspective. A critical consciousness is finally a dynamic tension between the interpreter's own singular take on the world, and a broader view of that same world as canonized or legitimated by a panoply of external forces, whether social, aesthetic, institutional, and so on. My starting thesis is that the critique of an ethnic group is no longer tenable owing to the fact that identity itself, the pinnacle of Modernity in both science and philosophy, is no longer a neatly contoured value in a post-modern social world. Moreover, fields which employed the notion, such as ethnic, race, and gender studies, have also shown to have such amorphous boundaries as to invite a reconsideration of their principles and objectives. Scholars and thinkers such as Werner Sollors, Richard Alba, Paul Gilroy, Jean Baudrillard, and Judith But-

[1] A shorter version of this paper was presented at the conference "For a Dangerous Pedagogy: A Manifesto for Italian and Italian American Studies," Hofstra, Columbia, and New York Universities, April 14–17, 2010.

From: *Transcending Borders, Bridging Gaps* (Calandra Institute, 2015)

ler, among others, have suggested in their different ways that we may be unwittingly cultivating forms of adversarial critique which in the end perpetuate the structures they were intended to combat. Let us look at some master tropes from the point of view of their inner dissolution.

There is no unitary transcendent identitarian trait to being American. Historically, "we the people" have invented for ourselves and paraded for decades the American Adam and then the American Aeneas, we have had the Imperial Self and the Nativist Self, the Great Liberators and the Great Society, we claimed to have defined the American Century and, most recently, invented the presumptuous ideology of imposing a New World Order to some six billion plus people. But which America is the "real one?" And is there just "one America"? Just compare a history of America written by Daniel Boorstin with one written by Howard Zinn. Some thirty years ago Benedict Anderson made the point: national identity is a rhetorical invention, an imaginary construct. Not that this makes it any the less real, and absolves us from confronting what these mega-ideologies perpetrate on the social structure. A century earlier, in the hey-day of nationalism, Ernst Renan had made a similar point, implicitly calling for awareness and commitment: a nationality is a daily plebiscite. The Italian American community should understand that whatever they call their identity is an ideology that imposes itself for a certain period of time and then is substituted by another, because each hegemonic discourse lasts just so long as it can muster the production and management of meaning. In a sense, we are constantly on the verge of not having achieved an identity, and of having achieved more than one over the course of time. This applies to sub- or anti-hegemonic discourse as well, so the gripes of Italian Americans during World War I, and in the late-sixties/early-seventies ("I'm proud to be Italian" days), and then for affirmative action in the eighties and for entry into the literary canon in the nineties: well, those too may have seen their better, or more useful, days.

If, on my theory, we should also go beyond dichotomic, dualistic thinking, and stop playing this game of saying I am proud of my heritage but I am of course American, or, otherwise stated, I am an American with a difference, which precedes the hyphen (or the slash), because at some point—say, when you pay your taxes or apply for a visa or are sent to war—you will have to deny the adjective; then Italian Americans should bear in mind that they are constitutively threatened to have to relinquish one part of their selves when certain contingencies arise. Yet, at the same, they also should remember that they have the advantage of being both inside and outside of America, or what America thinks of itself at any given point in time (i.e., during elections, financial crises, or educational reforms).

If there is no unitary national discourse that can credibly reveal where the essence (horrible word!) of this identitarian trait resides, then to speak of Italianness is even more perplexing, and rather than citing Antonio Gramsci about the failed conjunction between nation and state, or nation and people, I would point you toward an anthropological history of Italy even before a political one. Never really united and constantly traversed and inseminated by countless invaders and abused by all sorts of rulers and *most poignantly by their own kind*, the substrate of Italy inscribes an infinite palimpsest of the most diverse cultural forms and linguistic habits. To claim being Italian is to claim, paradoxically, the right not to absolute identity but rather to perennial differences or worse to pragmatic indifference vis-à-vis the big causes and the grand schemes. It is conducive to a solipsistic mental anarchy. How many different conceptions of Italy do Italian Americans cultivate, propagandize, and demand respect for? Some know it as tourists, some in nostalgic terms, while others downright concoct themselves a long bygone paradise, a classical, classy, romanticized utopia. Among those who have studied it, there is no quarter either, for the idea and description of a "mother country" or "country of the ancestors" cannot be separated from their ideological and political world view, as well as from the methods adopted to study the subject in the first place.

Nevertheless, my entreat is that Italian Americans must make good on what is clearly becoming a privileged perspectival locus, that is, being *both*, inside (symbolically, historically) *and* outside (geo-socially, legally) Italy.

The critical task is then the following: take advantage of our *intellectual situatedness* in the mare magnum of both, American and Italian cultural milieus, as practically emarginated and often demonstrably invisible to whatever is the dominant notion of mainstream. The reason is that to become mainstream means ultimately to be leveled, homogenized, made to speak and act in predictable ways. Perhaps to be *hyphenated* is not, or no longer, a bad place to be. Recent critics speak in fact of *living the border*, critically and pedagogically inhabiting the fault line, capitalizing on being able to see both sides at the same time, challenging the platitudes, forcing rethinking on any one issue that wishes to be definitive and finite.

The notion of critique at/from the margin is bolstered if we accept a key theoretical premise: *we are all migrants*, as people are constantly on the move: migrations are not mere epiphenomena suitable for sociological tabulations or economic theses and useful only during political campaigns. We are always on the move—socially, existentially, educationally. In terms of class, in view of the places we live in and communities we deal with, on the basis of our perspective, our reading of the world and the societies within it, are constantly shifting. Some people do not notice, some people do not want to notice, but the *world of cultures* never stands still. It may in fact be necessary to think of *worlds of culture*, not unusually co-existing at the same time and place and often unbeknownst of one another.

Key critical topos to be added is the notion of *métissage*, cross-breeding or miscegenation, inspired in part by studies on Central and South America and the Indian subcontinent, and to which scholars such as Serge Gruzinski, Walter Mignolo, Homi Bhabha, Eduard Glissant, Carmen Bernand, Armando Gnisci and others have given a philosophical and political value. Historically, the offspring of invasion, colonization, and exploitation, and formerly tainted by shame, in post-colonial times the *métisse, el mestizo* has become a proud identitarian quality with which to resist or implicitly critique the homogenizing, universalizing, and imperious Northern European white man's ideal with his science of numbers and taxonomy ready to box everyone in their place.

Along the same lines we find the recent critical *figura*, that of *hybridity*. In recent decades the hybrid—the person as well as the concept—has witnessed and finally acknowledged that he or she has gone from an unwanted, or invisible, or instrumentalized subaltern to a self-affirming and defiant multidimensional individual, politically slippery and existentially complex. *Hybrid* has several meanings: 1) Technically, it is "the offspring of two animals or plants of different races, breeds, varieties, species or genera." Think of mules or fuchsia flowers. 2) A resemanticization of the word in specific semiotic environments gives us the recently acquired meaning of "something—such as a power plant, vehicle, or electronic circuit—that has two different types of components performing the same function." One can think of the Prius as of diesel-electric locomotives. 3) Figuratively, it means "a person whose background is a blend of two diverse cultures or traditions." 4) Metaphorically, it signifies "something heterogeneous in origin or composition."

Consider now point 3. In terms of descent, every region or province in Italy has been witness to countless invasions and occupations—Calabria alone can document over thirty distinct ethnic groups! Thus culturally, despite diachronically circumscribed periods lasting anywhere from one to three centuries, Italians are a distillation of the most diverse backgrounds: people from Pakistan to Morocco, from Wales to Egypt, from the Normans (in turn from Scandinavia, the Vikings) and Schwabians (southern Germany) to the Carthagenians (Tunisia; in turn from Lebanon), from the Tartars to various Slavs, from the Albanians to the Turks to the much revered Greeks, to mention the most easily recognizable, have traveled and dwelled on the peninsula. And when on Italian soil, they came into contact—or conflict, or exchange—with autochthonous peoples, indeed tribes (the closest thing to Amerindian "Indian nations") called Brettii, Lucani, Ausoni, Samnites, Itali, Latini, Oscans, Etruscans, Liguri, and others further North, in the Padania and Sub-Alpine territories, which had already been settled by Celts, the Huns, and various strands of Goths. Each of these *ethnos* left an indelible mark in any one of the many semiotic fields a culture exhibits at any one point in time. In light of concrete historical facts, considering oneself Italian therefore is reduced to a) diachronically, which ancestors one *chooses* to be their signal noble forebears, and b) synchronically, one's idea of what Italy is, or better, and more accurately, *wishes* it to be, there being countless counter-examples to prove any claim erroneous or biased. Perhaps the scathing remark made by Prince Metternich of Austria before the 1848 revolution that "Italy is a geographical expression" has still a slight bitter ring of truth … at least at the time. But a less quirky observation is to relate the awareness of the stratified composition of Italianness to Vico's notion that "all nations have noble ancestry" and update it with the existential-political idea that it is we, the human actors, who decide who the noble ancestors are. This may include people whom we might want to forget, but should not precisely because they orient us toward what actually took place. Italian history is replete with exclusions, the forgotten and "worthless," just as it is chock-full of great inventors, navigators, saints, artists and entrepreneurs when it comes time to boast and unfurl proudly the national colors. But *the theoretical conclusion is that Italians (as "nationals" from any country) are all hybrids, creoles, mestizos to some degree.* The task of critique is to ask which ones, and why at some point in time and place, have claimed *not* to be hybrid, vaunting an invented purity or exclusivity, and to whose disadvantage. Anyone who begins a discussion claiming that they are "authentic Italians" (or authentic anything) has forfeited the right to an historical and critical analysis. For in so doing, such an individual precludes the possibility of a critical perspective, and therefore prevents any possibility of dialogue and/or self-examination, thereby positioning him/herself as *the* authority, the legitimate bearer of something that, I contend, is impossible or negatively biased.

And yet, the useful and revealing post-identitarian hybrid also has been coopted by end-of-millennium technocapitalism. Just consider the evolution of advertising strategies over the past quarter of a century: be different, think outside of the box, follow no one, etc. When it comes to merchandising, somehow being different, being of mixed extraction is fine, interesting, in fact constitutive of a certain idea of America! But scholars have also shown how the techniques of persuasion of the contemporary mega-machine of advertising and consensus-gathering has fine-tuned strategies first developed under authoritarian regimes, with Nazism and Fascism perfecting them to an art. Even the cognate concept of *creolization* is now employed as a marketing tool! What I submit we should counter foist to this domestication is rather the idea of *syncretism*. This latter is a notion, another critical *figura*, that strengthens topological critique, in urgent need of attention and development. Cultural anthropologists have already isolated a conscious and an unconscious syncretism, a permanent versus a transitional syncretism, and of course a subjective versus an objective type.

This reality-based paradigm applies as well to the Americans, whose founding myth was inscribed by overzealous religious refugees ostracized by even more intolerant monarchies on both side of the Channel. It took a few centuries and much blood spilled to accept, at least before the law of the land, that certain other "races" were also entitled to the same national rights and protection. In the heyday of the great Amerindian genocide, Americans were simultaneously proud to accept the "wretched of the earth" from all over the globe. It is well known that the America of Manifest Destiny did in the end succeed in creating a dominant cohesive identity even as two other forms of discourse emerged alongside it, in clear opposition to one another: One was the burgeoning nationalist/imperialist ideology, which we can date to the end of the nineteenth century and which exploded after the Second World War; the other a discourse of the other, the immigrant, that either caved in to coopting assimilation or was to be ghettoized for maintaining some of form of local and/or limited cultural identity. It did work for some groups, slowly, painfully, but not when the "others" in the amalgam were visibly different (Africans, Asians). And today still, a look at the breakdown of the recent census reveals that the "true" American is a conceptual invention, a necessary trope, a changeable identifier whose substance is defined by who is in power and controls the means of production and reproduction of ideologemes and stereotypes. Thus the longest surviving republic in world history has been successful in its meandering parade of self-aggrandizing mythologies in creating two hydra-like powerful narratives not always compatible with each other: one well known and ingrained at the micrological level, says: *e pluribus unum*; the other we could call: *Caveant peregrini* (loosely, Foreigners watch out!). A few more remarks are necessary to flesh out the topic.

The first mythology we have heard *ad nauseam*: rehashing the founding ideal of One [country, or people] from the Many, by the end of the nineteenth century it morphed into the fabled and problematic discourse of the melting pot, "the fires of God round His Crucible." Ironically, it was an immigrant Russian Jew, Israel Zangwill, who created the expression—from the homonymous 1908 play—that, honest ideals notwithstanding, became a banner for a growing conformist social politics: Deracination and forgetting the past were prerequisite to total assimilation into America-the future. But concurrent with this larger scheme there was a movement to re-launch a particular type of the ideal American, one which, to legitimate its origins, located the prototype in a white North-European Protestant, preferably Anglo-Saxon. But not many looked up where the Anglo-Saxon came from: a marauding hodgepodge from the entrails of medieval North-East Europe who invaded Britain when the Roman Empire collapsed, and were in turn followed by Danes and other Germanic tribes. In any case, a look at the Dillingham Commission volumes, published in 1908, will be revealing: The America of the post-Civil War era, of the Statue of Liberty, in other words, is not the America of the World War I years. But another crucial point in this national allegory, which is not fully explored here but is certainly in the background and fuel for future researches, is the thesis that even *before* the melting pot ideal there has always been at work a process of selection and exclusion of who might be admitted to the new experiment in democracy, veined as it was with utopian tendencies and biblical mirages (think of all the New Jerusalem utopias of the nineteenth century) concurrent with very strong prejudices toward four-fifths of the world's population. On this thesis, submitted by Aristide Zolberg, it was never true that this country readily accepted anyone and everyone, Crevencour and Toqueville notwithstanding. The claim is that above and beyond actual federal immigration law and other supporting local policies (and often as a result of them), the ruling elites in Washington and the Northeast have consistently manifested, though most times in tacit ways, a penchant for favoring the arrival and incorporation of the well-bred, the blue-bloods, the megacapitalists. The melting pot ideal, imposed as it was on the later immigrants until they themselves, or at least their children, spontaneously embraced it, turned out to be a useful ideologeme to train against and regiment locally the seeming unstoppable tides of foreigners arriving on these shores at the beginning of the twentieth-century, then after the Second World War, and now again at the beginning of the twenty-first.

When identity is no longer a case of A = A, and its negation is no longer A = not-A, then we might consider what happens when A = B, C, D,...*n*! Plainly stated, we are possessors and merchants of identities, in the plural, each assuming a temporally marked and socially circumscribed form in view of the given interlocutors, as remarked at the outset. Most recently, William McNeill, Clifford Geertz and Chäim Perelman have in specific ways enlightened us on this process. Identity is constructed, negotiated time and again in public arenas (whether in the conference hall, on TV networks, at Board of Directors' meetings, etc.). It depends intrinsically on *the rhetoric of the occasion*, in view of a constantly restaged confrontation requiring flexibility, dialogue, new syntheses, reconfigured programmes. Along with this then should go the principle that a *relative* sense of equality across ethnic, racial, and gender lines is required solely before the law of the land. But that too is never absolute: that is why we have public debates, law courts, and amendments to the Constitution.

Therefore, *if* Italian American gender, race, and identity studies over the past twenty plus years have exposed the inconsistencies of the Italian American family for both being incapable of shedding the Ancient ways of rural Italy *and* for being unable to see the paradoxes that lurk beneath the contemporary American Mainstream middle-class paradigm, *then* perhaps their engagement should consider a number of alternative arguments or, in my vocabulary, *topoi*.

First of all, we need to abandon the rhetoric of contradiction and accusation, as it is essentialist and conducive to an antagonistic dichotomy against which there is no point arguing, for one will have to employ the same strategies, the same sequence of demonstrations, as the opponent. Without bothering Aristotle on this, in current critical metalanguage Lyotard demonstrated in *Le Différend* that the resolution to an argument is provided by the one who has performative power, the one who can act upon his or her words. Fortunately, in democratic regimes, there are always means to re-enter the arena or the assembly and try different forms of persuasion, leverage other topoi, engage previously unused or underutilized techniques, offices, services, alliances, legal provisions, master tropes, educational support and, why not, political influence.

And yet, one has constantly to bear in mid the larger picture and grasp the paradox of equality, and prod further: equal to what? to whom? Who/what establishes the norm, the democratically acceptable baseline? Recent studies have dumped the linear model of assimilation into a vaguely defined mainstream by immigrants and minorities and have drawn instead attention to the variety and complexity of *sites of cultural negotiation*, tactics of survival and the creative refashioning of identities more in terms of *local consent* than of mythical descent, more in terms of flows than of structures. For Certain aspects of one's idea of his/her "sense of being" (as opposed to "identity") can be transacted, modified, talked about, shaped into something else. Identities and differences being therefore both malleable and necessarily amorphous, the real battleground that looms ever more menacing is now (as perhaps always was) located in the business and the political world, in the obstinate persistence of a class struggle paradigm that all nations and peoples seem to have experienced, and in the historically recent discourse of the cross-group, trans-national arena of ecology and the environment, both of which rephrase how we conceive basic needs like energy and food that impact on the greater society as a whole. How many Italian Americans, critics as writers, filmmakers as artists, lawyers as business people, engaged these arenas of contention and *not* be coded by ethnic, national, or linguistic signs that bespeak "identitarian" markers? And is this something that can be done? That we as a community should do? As the writer Victor Magiar suggested, it is time we stop speaking of ethnic identity and think in terms of cultural identity, which is clearly more comprehensive, less prone to be appropriated by pseudoscientists, and apt at revealing a broader palette of these sites of negotiation and connexed rhetorics of empowerment.

What is left to be done must be conducted in view of the larger dynamics of America as a whole and how its manifold if self-contradictory ideologies stretch their tentacles in ever more insidious ways all over the globe, absorbing and recycling forms of discourse that claim specificity, authenticity, exclusivity. Thus even gender, race, and identity politics must be linked again and perhaps primarily to *class struggle*, indeed to the dynamics of capital, for if we pay heed to the social developments of the last half century, and in particular to the demise of the bi-polar world system, all three critical approaches—which have of course opened our eyes to a plethora of problems—have become somewhat calcified and liable to instrumental academic maneuvering suitable to pit one group against another: the classic approach to ruling: *divide et impera*! Once a privilege of emperors and monarchs, adopted by the military the world over, this approach is now the lifeblood of that collusion between capital and state, between investors, state officials and university functionaries. These are known to the Foucauldians as discursive formations, sanctioned phraseologies that admit certain issues to be mentioned in public while others are excluded. A different philosophical school would consider them language games devised by those trans-national, multi-ethnic, supra-gendered coalitions running governments and corporations which require that each subgroup, each category be assigned a place and a role, given limited space to move and speak so that its constituent component members can in the end be controlled like figurines. The diabolical aspect of this state of affairs is that those in control of the levers of power no longer practice zero-sum games: that was the case when one could see and identify the opponent, devise a plan of attack, conceive of a strategy of resistance. Not in the twenty-first century! As seen, rut resistance too seems to have been coopted. In the age of non-zero sum games, even the losers are made to believe they have won something. Just think of the corporate strategy of firing union workers and then re-hiring them at a lower pay without benefits, and send the message around that the economy is picking up, that unemployed are entering the labor market, etc.

If there is going to be a change in how marginal, minorities, and immigrants are represented and granted access to the various social and symbolic infrastructures of a liberal society, it cannot come by "resisting" from the outside, as it were, but by making it to the level where certain decisions are made. This is implicitly pleading a case for the cruciality of education: today's young are the only hope. We must provide the critical and socio-economic means that allow these new generations access to the loci of power, in the hope that when they do get the opportunity to sit at the table with the powers that be, say, to launch a certain campaign or promote a certain product, they can question, analyze and suggest solutions that are good not only for this or that group, but first of all for all groups, and regions, and cultures, and then, of course, negotiate the specificity at hand because places and locales is where humans actually dwell and interact concretely.

The fact that then in the name of personal glory, hubris or pecunia some so-called representative figures of a given social group do not intervene against and, as often is the case, willy-nilly contribute to the persistence and amplification of well-worn but still offensive stereotypes about *their own* background, well, there is little one can do: it goes with living in a democracy. But we can begin by recalibrating our critical instruments, devise an alternative form of critique, begin to write a counter-history, create the archive we still don't have, open up our field of interest to thematics not immediately marked by ethnicity, nationality, or language, even there where these can still be addressed and provide, methodologically, inroads onto broader issues.

We must learn from our historical past as immigrants and refashion ourselves as perennial political and critical migrants inhabiting the interstices of post-industrial, post-national societies. We must adopt a different rhetoric, be flexible and quick enough to accept, wear, and market our many identities to our advantage. We must discard the logic of opposition and antagonism and espouse a rhetoric of cautiously embracing the endlessly distorted systems of aggregation and legitimation of power. We must rather get *inside* the system and *willingly* become invisible while remembering that "no man is an island," that the *en-soi* exists *avec les autres*, that the *Mit-Sein* (being-with) establishes the very foundation of *Da-sein*, where by itself it can only utter oracles. The only caveat, the sole precategorical imperative, the lone golden rule that may be valid through time, space, and consciousness, is that one does not put the life of someone else in peril. I don't know of any major ancient or modern ethical, religious, or political narrative that is grounded upon violence against other human beings (which is not to say they do not address the question of war). Beyond that, given that any ideology, any discursive formation, and any identitarian programme can be made to be valid and normative at some point in some context, above and beyond any consideration of an absolute truth, what we are left with is the potential to re-invent our identities many times over in the endless exchanges that take place as we move through social structures and symbolic systems, as we literally migrate—move on—in our day to day activities, through forests of signs, archipelagoes of meaning, deserts of vacuous advertising, dodging the savannahs of *kleptoplutocracy*.

From the general dustbin of history we need to recover—and modify it to function within this centerless continuously destabilized social continuum—the notion of the self-created *consciousness of relation within delimited horizons*, that is to say, the manifold localized fields of interaction. We must try to understand ourselves as beings who are constantly reinterpreting who they are, who have at once the humbleness and fearlessness to accept that there is no supratemporal or transhistorical ego or identity, and yet believe that lives make sense primarily on the basis of a positive and encouraging exchange with someone else who is also looking to determine the key values of the *common-place* inhabited. We need to learn to sympathize and dis-course with people who have been mentally and socially colonized but who have realized that everyone to some degree is colonized, power relations notwithstanding.... Or should we say, power relations being the proof of the validity of the statement that we need continuously to redefine ourselves. A good deal of this scantily sketched ethic is to be found in Pasolini's *Lutheran Letters*, a collection of columns published as his last great work, where one can read of an idea of brotherhood which is neither Christian nor Italian, nor French!—just plain human.

One final concern is the fact that despite this sea of woes, this ongoing deveining of all critical schools, in the heart of the imploding empire, in the throes of the Orwellian distortion, even as knowledge is perennially unstable, constantly reconfigured, translated from medium to medium, suppressed or misused mercilessly, and sold to anyone who can come up with the required capital, in the face of all this, I say we must create or salvage the archive of our experience. There are problems and dangers with such an enterprise, no doubt, but the principle of hope here is that even in a world as bleakly depicted, almost a prologue to our times, by Ray Bradbury in *Fahrenheit 451*, and perhaps precisely because of it, we must make sure that future generations know, or at least have available somewhere somehow, the texts, the founding texts, the words of their fathers and mothers. This means also their transmission and mutations, the words that tried to capture the experience of the generations, the ever-renewing archai of our shifty socio-historical realities. For if no one hears the tree fall in the forest, it might as well never have fallen. If the document, the evidence, cannot be found, the case for a historical memory that enriches our present social interactions cannot be made. And the memory (even if on a hard-disk, even if in the "cloud"!) will be empty. Italian Americans, as any group that considers itself marginalized, underrepresented, or unjustly wiped off the master discourse of the national allegory, must make sure their own past does not become white noise, or worse just blank silence: existence and self-validation require memory, social collective memory, an archipelago of perspectives linked to it uneven and partly unknown archeology where one can retrieve, re-interpret and if relevant or desired rewrite one's sense of being in the world today.

The D'Amato Chair in Italian Studies at Stony Brook University launched such an initiative in 2009. Titled "The Italian American Archive Project," details can be gleaned at the following website: http://www.peter carravetta.com/italian-american-archive. It would require a team of researchers, experts on creating web-platforms, an established publisher, hyper-text search engines, and so on, not excluding availability in multi-volume book format and e-book. But basically it needs capital! The ultimate stimulus for a would-be Maecenas to step up and support such an enterprise would derive not only from the felt need to create "our own" historical memory, but from the added consideration that it would serve to non-Italians and non-Italian Americans if and when they need to speak about anything regarding this group. The point here is that when a journalist, an anchor, a scholar, a young researcher looking to write a thesis, someone from a different country, and so on encounters the expression Italian American, they have to rely on skimpy information, platitudes and hearsay. If we have the documentation philologically accurate and professionally prepared, then at least we can rectify some misconceptions, while adding to the circulation of knowledge, facts and figures temporarily forgotten. And when someone exaggerates or falsifies certain representations, we would then have a basis to contest, or to invite to a dialogue, and have a fair shot at persuading them that matters are much more complex, that social history is a fluid and problematic continuum, that new interpretations are possible. And that perhaps the Italian Americans can help in understanding America, Italy, the migration and incorporation process, and so on.

ESSENTIAL BIBLIOGRAPHY

Anderson, Benedict. *Imagined Communities: Reflections on the Origin and Spread of Nationalism*. London: Verso, 1983.

Anderson, Quentin. *The Imperial Self.* New York: Vintage, 1971.

Appadurai, Arjun. "Disjunction and Difference in the Global Cultural Economy." *Public Culture*, II, 2, Spring (1990).

Alba, Richard. *Italian Americans: Into the Twilight of Ethnicity*. New York: Prentice Hall, 1984.

Bade, Klaus J. *Europa in Bewegung: Migration von späten 18 Jahrhundert bis zur Gegenwart*. Transl. M. García Garmilla. Barcelona: Critica, 2003.

Baudrillard, Jean. *Selected Writings*. Transl. M. Poster. Stanford: Stanford UP, 2001.

Bernand, Carmen, and Serge Gruzinski, *Historia del Nuevo Mundo, II: los mestizajes (1550-1640)*. Mexico, DF, Fondo de Cultura Economica, 2005.

Bhabha, Homi, ed., *Nation and Narration*. New York: Routledge, 1990.

Boorstin, Daniel. *The Americans*. 3 vols. New York: Vintage Books, 1958, 1965, 1973.

Butler, Judith. *Undoing Gender*. New York, Routledge, 2004.

Carravetta, Peter. *The Elusive Hermes. Method, Discourse, Interpreting*. Aurora (CO): Davies Group Publishers, 2013.

_______."Migration, History and Existence," in V. Kyriakopoulos, ed., *Migrants and Refugees*. Athens : Komotini, 2004:19-50.

Castles, Stephen, and Mark J. Miller, eds. *The Age of Migration: International Population Movements in the Modern World*. New York: Guilford Press, 1993.

Ciuffoletti, Zeffiro and Maurizio Degl'Innocenti, eds. *L'emigrazione nella storia d'Italia 1868/1975*. Firenze: Vallecchi, 1978.

Clifford, James and George Marcus, eds. *Writing Culture: the Poetics and the Politics of Ethnography*. Berkeley: U California P, 1986.

Foucault, Michel. *The Archaelogy of Knowledge & The Discourse on Language*. Engl. transl. by A.M. Sheridan Smith. New York, Harper & Row, 1976.

Geertz, Clifford. *The Interpretation of Cultures*. New York, Basic Books, 2000 [1973].

Gilroy, Paul. *Against Race. Imagining Political Culture Beyond the Color Line*. Cambridge (MA): Harvard UP, 2000.

Gnisci, Armando. *We, the Europeans*. Transl. M. Rusnack. Aurora (CO): Davies Group Publishers, 2014.

Gruzinski, Serge. *La pensée métisse*. Paris: Fayard, 1999.

Hobsbawn, Eric, and Terence Ranger, eds. *The Invention of Tradition*. Cambridge (UK): Cambridge UP, 1983.

Hoerder, Dirk. *Cultures in Contact. World Migrations in the Second Millennium*. Durham: Duke UP, 2001.

Ilari, Virgilio. *Inventarsi una patria: Esiste un'identità nazionale?* Roma: Ideazione, 1996.

Irigaray, Luce. *Key Writings*. New York, Continuum, 2004.

Lyotard, Jean-François. *Le Différend*. Paris, Minuit, 1983.

McNeill, William. *Polyethnicity and National Unity in World History*. Toronto: U Toronto, 1985.

Nancy, Jean-Luc. *Identity*. Transl. F. Raffoul. New York : Fordham UP, 2015.

Pasolini, Pier Paolo. *Lutheran Letters*. Engl. Transl. S. Hood. Carcanet P, 1987.

Pilger, John. *The New Rulers of the World*. London: Verso, 2002.

Said, Edward. *The World, The Text, The Critic*. Cambridge, Harvard UP, 1983.

Sartre, Jean-Paul. *What is Literature?* Transl. H. Barnes. New York: Colophon, 1972.

Shields, John C. *The American Aeneas. Classical Origins of the American Self*. Knoxville: U Tennessee P, 2001.

Sollors, Werner. *Beyond Ethnicity*. New York, Oxford University Press, 1986.

Starobinski, Jean. *L'oeil vivant II. La relation critique*. Paris, Gallimard, 1970.

Steinberg, Stephen. *The Ethnic Myth: Race, Ethnicity, and Class in America*. Boston: Beacon P, 1981.

Tabori, Paul. *The Anatomy of Exile: A Semantic and Historical Study*. London: Harrap, 1972.

Vico, Giambattista. *New Science*. Transl. D. Marsch. New York, Penguin, 1999.

Waldenfels, Bernhard. *Topologie de l'étranger*. Transl. F. Gregorio et al. Paris: Van Dieren Ēditeur, 2009.

Wallerstein, Immanuel. *The Modern World-System*, 2 vols. New York: Academic P, 1974-82.

Zeidel, Robert. *Immigrants, Progressives, and Exclusion Politics: the Dillingham Commission, 1900-1927*. De Kalb (IL): Northern Illinois UP, 2004.

Zinn, Howard. *A People's History of the United States*. New York: HarperCollins, 2003.

Zolberg. Aristide R. *A Nation by Design. Immigration Policy in the Fashioning of America*. New York: Russell Sage Foundation, 2006.

Typologies for a New Perspective on the Italian-American Body Politic Presenting the Oral History Archive

Ottorino Cappelli
University of Naples, "L'Orientale"

Politics and government represent the missing piece of Italian-American studies, and one that we need to put back in place as rapidly as possible. While there exist a few historical and biographical accounts of Italian-American politicians, very little study has been produced by students of social sciences about how they operate. One of the reasons for this is that very little primary sources exist for scholars to examine. By founding the Oral History Archive, we at the John D. Calandra Italian American Institute have started to fill this gap.

Now named in memory of Maria Federici—an Italian parliamentarian and a member of the Constituent Assembly (1946–48), as well as the founder of ANFE (Associazione Nazionale Famiglie degli Emigranti)—the Archive focuses its activity on the detailed study of elected officials of Italian origin, and endeavor that includes a series of in-depth televised interviews with each of them. The first bulk of these interviews, which is now available both as a video series and as a book, represents a unique foundation of primary sources for scholars and students of American and Italian-American politics.[1]

There are two ways to describe the subject of this research. First, at the most immediate level, it is the Italian-American experience in New York as told by those members of the community who have been successful in one particular social realm: the running for and the holding of elective of-

---

[1] Up to now, the Oral History Archive has collected some forty hours of video-taped conversations with twenty elected officials of Italian origin who serve or have served in the legislative body of the State of New York, the Assembly and the Senate. These interviews are presented in abridged form in my *Italians in Politics in America. Conversations with Italian-American Legislators of the State of New York* (New York: John D. Calandra Italian American Institute, 2015). The book was co-produced by ANFE and funded in part by a grant from the Ministero degli Affari Esteri e della Cooperazione Internazionale.

From: *Transcending Borders, Bridging Gaps* (Calandra Institute, 2015)

fice. On a broader level, the subject is American politics per se, in particular, in New York, as seen through the eyes of one of its most numerous single components, Americans of Italian ancestry.

A cursory look at some numbers may give a better idea of the quantitative relevance of the subject. According to official 2010 Census estimates, close to eighteen million Americans claim direct Italian ancestry (5.6 percent of the U.S. population); in the State of New York they are more than two and a half millions (13.5 percent). The New York Conference of Italian-American State Legislators, in turn, has approximately forty-five members out of a total of 213 legislators. With one member out of five, the Italian Americans of New York are clearly over-represented in the legislature. Or, looking at the same phenomenon from another perspective, one-fifth of the population of New York (about four million people) is represented by an Italian-American elected official. Not to speak, of course, of the executive branch, where Governor Andrew Cuomo is now in his second term, two decades after his father left the same office, the late Mario Cuomo, an icon of American—and not just Italian-American—politics.

Americans of Italian ancestry, in sum, are an integral part of the American social fabric and an admirably successful component of its political class. This should not come as a surprise; for the American political system was conceived, since the nineteenth century, as a machine to integrate immigrants. Those who lacked two essential components of social power—wealth and status—would resort to politics, provided they had the necessary resources of numbers and skills. Lacking the former and having plenty of the latter, Italian immigrants seized the day. And, today's anti-political sentiments notwithstanding, the formation of an Italian-American political class provided a crucial, albeit often unrecognized contribution to the advancement of their community at large.

To my knowledge, no one summed up this process better than former New York State Senator James Alesi during our interview for the Archive, when told us that,

> [G]overnment was the vehicle that brought Italian Americans into mainstream America. Some of them were professionals … but … those who were not professionals, like my father, they grew socially … because many of them were in government. That's how they elevated themselves and gave themselves credibility in their own community. It is really the

> opportunity to run for office that, I believe, elevated the Italian Americans ... that was the one thing that allowed you to gain status without being a professional.

All this, however, did not come without a struggle. And this is why our interviews dwell at length upon the early part of our protagonists' life: their growing up in close-knit ethnic communities, usually in urban areas; their developing a passion for politics, often through their family or closest friends; their first steps in the political arena, supported as a rule by networks of fellow ethnics. And once they get to this point, more often than not, we see a corollary of ethnic tensions and frictions, especially with the Irish, which accompanies their attempt to establish an Italian presence in American politics.

In this, our protagonists show more similarities than differences among themselves. Most of them share similar experiences in their primary political socialization, whether they come from New York City or from upstate, whether they are young or old, male or female, Democrats or Republicans, and whether they originate from a political family (sometimes even a local dynasty). Their individual stories, in other words, confirm a collective history of the Italians in America that sounds familiar—especially from literary accounts—though adding fascinating personal details that expand our knowledge and understanding of the role of ethnicity in American politics.

But it is when we follow them throughout their political career, from their first successful campaigns to the subsequent consolidation of their power and influence, that interesting differences start to emerge, offering a more articulated, complex picture of their politics. This is no place to dwell on these findings, but I will briefly sketch them out, in order to give an idea of what the Oral History Archive has achieved so far. In a few words, what we found is that there are four different typologies of Italian-American politicians, each dealing with the ethnic issue from a different angle. Few of our interviewees fit completely and exclusively one of these typologies, and many would exhibit elements of some or even all of them, but each sports some predominant type of political behavior—or, at the very least, of political rhetoric—that relates to one or the other of the following ideal-types.

The *Party Champion.* This type of politician shows a strong sense of party loyalty and emphasizes party identification over ethnic identity.

Most of those in this typology are Democrats who grew up politically in New York City and other urban areas at a time when Republicans were virtually non-existent and the Democrats hegemonic. As Italians, they endured harsh battles within their party to become accepted as potential candidates for office; they had to confront and ultimately replace their party leaders, who most often were Irish. So the ethnic element is there, undoubtedly. Yet when it comes to their appeal in general elections, the Party Champions would stress organizational loyalty and class representation over ethnic belonging, urging members of all ethnic groups to identify as Democrats and vote down the party line. This typology does not make a uniform bloc, however, and the reader of this book will find such type of cross-ethnic, party-political discourse among both conservative-leaning Democrats and progressive-leaning Democrats—or, if I may submit an Italian-centered label for the latter, "Mario Cuomo Democrats."

The *Ethnic Politician* is the mirror opposite of the Party Champion, except that this typology too is found mainly in urban areas with a high concentration of immigrants and a predominance of registered Democrats. But elected officials in this category are mostly Republicans who, given the weakness of their party among the electorate of their district, must attempt to change the very rationale of how their constituents vote. Therefore, they encourage them to switch from disciplined (usually Democratic) party voting to cross-party ethnic voting. They will appeal first of all to Italian-American voters, irrespective of their party affiliation, by fostering ethic identity and pride and trying to turn them into powerful electoral drives. Elements of such rhetoric can be found among both liberal and conservative Republicans in our panel of interviewees—or, if I am allowed to continue with my Italian labeling exercise, among both "Giuliani" Republicans and "Al D'Amato" Republicans.

The *Value-Oriented Leader* may come in support of the second typology when the need arises to reinforce the ethnic-political identity of potential Italian voters or, and most interesting, when voters from other ethnicities need to be recruited in favor of an Italian candidate. The emphasis in this case will be on "traditional family values"—*traditional family* considered a quintessential Italian value, but one that also appeals to a number of other immigrant groups, from Hispanics to South Asians. Quite understandably, such rhetoric tends to be more typical of conservative-minded Republicans, often (but not exclusively) found in middle-class suburban areas. And it usually comes with a myriad of conservative stances, from anti-gay, pro-life, and (quite inconsequentially) pro-death-penalty positions, to less-tax, less-government messages. As the most influential politician to articulate this vision in our panel was Senator Serph Maltese, co-founder of the New York State Conservative Party, I would dub those in this category, "Maltese Conservatives."

It is true that the vast majority of our interviewees from whatever party, referred to family as a crucial value for Italian Americans—and, incidentally, the emphasis on the Italian immigrant family was also an element of Mario Cuomo's progressive discourse. But the value system of all Democrats in our group, both conservative- and liberal-leaning, bend primarily toward a pro-government, pro-welfare vision and often resort to a distinctive "wealth and business vs. the poor and those-in-need" kind of populist rhetoric. All of this is characteristically cross-ethnic and bears little peculiar relation to the Italian experience—except maybe for those more left-leaning like Senator Diane Savino, co-founder of the Working Families Party ("Marcantonio Progressives"?)

Finally, we have the *Local Interests Broker*, a typology that is actually omnipresent in American politics, irrespective of geography, party affiliation, and value systems. The electoral appeal of those in this category consists in their proven ability to deliver, to "bring the pork home." The typology is vast and embraces different sub-types, ranging from the old-style machine bosses, to more modern policy advocates who focus meticulously on constituents casework, to plainly non-political, managerial-style problem solvers. But, their differences notwithstanding, they all share an eminently distributive approach to politics and invariably couch it in the language of responsiveness, perceiving themselves as providers of the material needs of their voters.

This notably crowded group also differs internally under two other important respects. First, the power base of Local Interests Brokers may reside either in their party's political organization (in which case this typology may overlap with that of the Party Politician) or in a network of personal connections, often well rooted in a dynastic family fiefdom. Second, their capacity of ethnic outreach may vary according to whether they focus primarily on the interests and needs of their fellow ethnics (in which case this typology may overlap with that of the Ethnic Politician), or tend to care for all groups by flexibly adapting to the changing demographics of their districts. Although the vastness of this category hardly warrants a single label, Italian or not, I am tempted to suggest again "Al D'Amato," who in turn was famously dubbed "The Pothole Senator" and ostensibly took much pride in that.

It will not have escaped the reader that the above typologies are not peculiarly Italian—they identify different types of American politicians, independently of their ancestry. Yet, the fact that they took shape during our conversations with Italian-American legislators, and that we could easily find Italian names to label them and some of their sub-types, is in itself telling. What it reveals is that, having become an integral part of the American social fabric, the descendants of the Italian immigrants have generated a complex and internally differentiated body politics which is a microcosm of American politics and an excellent point of observation to study. This is, in fact, one of the most significant findings of our work, though hardly the only one.

I am confident that we are on the right track and that reading through the many pages of these first-hand narratives will make the journey as pleasant and fascinating for our readers as it was for us—the journey that brought the sons and daughters of Italian immigrants into positions of power and influence in their adoptive land.

THE "ITALIAN" WRITER
Reflections on a New Category

Anthony Julian Tamburri
JOHN D. CALANDRA ITALIAN AMERICAN INSTITUTE, QUEENS COLLEGE, CUNY

In his *Studi culturali*,[1] Michele Cometa maintains that migration literature—which, I would add, is analogous to ethnic literature in the United States—should not remain enclosed within either a "marginality" or an "exceptionality" of "such experiences" (97) in literature; this is a concept that I had already brought up elsewhere with regard to a different geo-cultural arena.[2] Now—"finally," I am happy to say—such an idea is being talked about in Italy as part of a theoretic discourse that is, one hopes, sufficiently widespread, despite the continuing resistance on the part of so many members of the Italian intellectual "establishment."

What Cometa goes on to say is true: that it is necessary to "compel Italianists to a reformulation of the canon and of canons partially put forward in recent decades" (97), broadening as a consequence, and as a necessity, the concept of "Italian identity," which currently is changing into something that goes beyond the traditional confines of that concept. An *effective identity*, therefore, in as much as it recognizes the quality of everyday activity in which the individual lives out his/her daily life; an *effective identity* also insofar as it recognizes what an individual does within a largely Italian milieu unfolds in that way specifically because he feels his actions to be done "Italian-ly" as part of his ordinary existence, and not in any honorary or *affected* sense, but actually "effective," such that whatever he does —and that he knows, as an Italian—is part of the life of every day of that person. And so, that "Italian effect" of his daily life is precisely that blending of Italian characteristics and/or *Italianistic-ness* of his identity.

What I am suggesting here echoes what Rebecca West wrote twenty-

---

[1] See his *Studi culturali* (Napoli: Guida, 2010).

[2] I direct the reader to my *To Hyphenate or not to Hyphenate: the Italian/American Writer: Or, An* Other *American?* (Montreal: Guernica Editions, 1991) *passim*, to my *A Semiotic of Ethnicity. In (Re-)cognition of the Italian/American Writer* (Albany, NY: SUNY P, 1998), chapter 7 *passim*, and to the essay by Aijaz Ahmad, "Jameson's Rhetoric of Otherness and the 'National Allegory'," *Social Text* 17 (1987), now in *In Theory* (London: Verso, 1992).

From: *Transcending Borders, Bridging Gaps* (Calandra Institute, 2015)

five years ago about a concept of Italian and/or Italian/American identity, of someone who is not by ethnic origin Italian, but who lives out her daily activities, be they professional or personal, if not specifically within, then at least for the most part close to what is coming to be called *Italianità*:[3]

> By bringing non-Italian or Italian/American perspectives to Italian literature and culture [...], we implicitly (and at times explicitly) question essentialist views of ethnicity. I could go so far as to say that I am, by dint of twenty-five years of study, scholarship, and professional engagement in Italian culture and literature, a kind of "Italian/American" (or "American/ Italian"). This identity is not to be found in my genes, my blood, or in any part of my material body, but rather in my orientation, my knowledge, and my commitment. [...] Similarly, adopted cultures may be seen in the same light as adopted children. If those children are more truly the children of their adoptive parents who nurture and cherish them than of their biological parents, then perhaps an adopted culture is eventually as much (or in some cases even more) "mine" as it is that of someone born into it. I recognize that I may never "feel" Italian or Italian/ American in the same way that natural sons and daughters of Italian culture may feel, but I would at the very least like to believe that my investment in that culture has marked me more than superficially as someone who is part of *italianità*. (337)[4]

If we accept just the very basics of what West is saying, that she in some way—and maybe on the strength of her "twenty-five years of study, research, and responsibilities having to do with Italian culture and literature"—belongs within the rather vast confines of *italianità*, we must then include in this world of *Italianità* also those who, while born and raised in Italy, live elsewhere, and in our case, in the United States.[5] And we can do

[3] For use of the slash (/) in place of the hyphen (-), see my *To Hyphenate* 43-47.

[4] "Scorsese's *Who's That Knocking At My Door?*: Night Thoughts on Italian Studies in the United States." *Romance Languages Annual*, Ben Lawton and Anthony Julian Tamburri, eds. (1991): 331-338.

[5] If we must enlarge further this concept of West's, we find ourselves in the end converging with the concept of "Italicity," which Piero Bassetti has been promulgating since 2002. He spoke about it first in his essay "Italicity: Global and Local", in *The Essence of Italian Culture and the Challenge of a Global Age*, edited by Paulo Ianni and George F. McLean (Washington, DC: The Council for Research in Vallues and Philosophy, 2002) 13-24, and he further elaborated it in *Italici. Il possibile futuro di una community globale* (Milano: Casagrande, 2008).

it fairly easily from the scientific point of view if we are disposed to break free of limiting, and dare I say arbitrary, confines and thus recognize instead that kaleidoscopic mosaic that is North America, as I classified it more than twenty-five years ago,[6] and that Cometa was correct when he said in his *Studi culturali* of the "migrant" writer: "The mosaic of identities that migrant writers carry around with them is much more complex and variegated," (107) as is even, as we have seen above, true in the case of someone like West. Following, then, such an intellectual trajectory with regard to migrant writers, writers of other classifications such as ethnicity, we nicely end up alongside the Bassettian discourse of "italics" and, in the broader sense of the concept, find ourselves confronted with an Italian world that surmounts every restrictive, reductive, and essentialist conceptual barrier.

LANGUAGE: "LOQUOR ERGO SUM"?

This everyday quality must by definition take into consideration the discourse of language, even or maybe because it is, in the most basic terms, the vehicle through which the writer communicates. Cometa talks about this in his *Studi culturali.* On this matter he tells us that "whether we're dealing with writing that *adopts* the Italian language or a culture that *refutes* it" (97; italics in the original) it is the second case that "will make it possible to draw with more clarity the identity map for literature that is made in Italy or, simply, that traverses Italy" (97).

I find rather curious the use of a verb like "traverse" for a literature that, although in a language other than the "national" one (an "other" language), is nonetheless always a literature conceived and written in that local context, which in this case would be one within Italian geo-cultural confines. It is precisely because of the problematics of language that in some way or other we have to take action; we can neither ignore it nor dismiss it as something trivial.[7] It is not simply a clear-cut matter, just to slightly re-

---

[6] I first addressed it in my *To Hyphenate* (1991) 48-51, and then in *Una semiotica dell'etnicità* (2010) 62-64.

[7] I direct the reader to the following studies that are blazing this trail for the first time in a profound manner: *Daniele Cambierati, Scrivere nella lingua dell'altro. La letteratura degli immigrati in Italia (1989-2007)* (Bern: Peter Lang, 2010); Armando Gnisci, "È ora di parlare di letteratura italiana. Se non ora, quando?", *e-scrita Revista do Curso de Letras da UNIABEU 2.4* (Jan.- Apr., 2011): 42-54, and his *Creolizzare l'Europa. Letteratura e migrazione* (Meltemi, 2003). These two essays are of great importance as manifestoes on the

phrase something Cometa says above. It is true that language is a vehicle, as we have already said, and, on the other hand, it is also true that language is the fundamental element by which one identifies oneself, in every sense of the word, and what it brings to mind for me (a small example, a skeptic might say) is the ethnic nomenclature for Americans of Italian origin.

I have already discussed the possible labels that may be used in dealing with "writers who came to the U.S., as adults, from Italy and who write in Italian"—yes, I have employed here a phrase that is impracticably long in speaking of U.S. writers of Italian. In my 2010 book, *Una semiotica dell'etnicità*, I had included under a single "Italian" umbrella both the writer who writes in English and the writer who writes in Italian. I wanted then, as I now do here, to avoid any terms that a) cut off the first representative term for the cultural inheritance of the person and that, b) uses a hyphen. I had wanted to shed light on the problem of the ethnic writer of Italian origin—and so I am not making a linguistic distinction—which is a classification that, for motives that are still obscure, has not been catalogued in a separate group where instead other ethnicities (and this seems to be true to this very day) are rightfully considered labels of merit, as seen from the outside, and of pride, as seen from the inside. I had proposed particularly for the adjective, as I continue to write today, both in Italian and English, the pairing "Italian/American"—a truly unattractive neologism, some would say. For the nominal form, on the other hand, I had proposed a term analogous to the American label, one that follows in turn Italian grammar, so that it becomes easy to refer to someone, in Italian, who is in the States but of Italian origin, as "americano italiano," as the equivalent of the English noun "Italian American." By so doing, the two terms retain their individual meanings in both forms—the adjectival and the nominal—and, for "ideological" reasons, the completeness of each socio-cultural term is simultaneously respected. Will it seem like a somewhat strange concept to an Italian reader to maintain the complete form of the first socio-cultural term in the formulation? Might it seem so on account of the fact that Italy has always been considered a monochromatic nation? It is beyond the scope of this essay to interrogate that kind of cultural phenomenon; I have already done this in both Italian and in English else-

---

fundamental changes we have been discussing with regard to the writer who writes in Italian while in the United States.

where.[8] In fact, examining such topics is, no doubt, most useful in moving forward with the goal of creating a sustained, multicultural Italian discourse, which, as I have said above, is a debate that has yet to catch on seriously in Italy.[9]

Luckily, together with Cometa's voice, there is Gnisci's thought on a similar issue. In his essay "It's Time to Talk about Italian Literature; If Not Now, When?" Gnisci discusses the situation of the writer of "migrant literature" (43) and his socio-cultural positioning in this rather vast field of the world of Italian literature and culture. Gnisci rejects *tout court* the idea of any kind of label:

> Labeling the phenomenon of contemporary Italophone literature, or of immigrant literature, or of burgeoning literature of the LIM [literature of Italian migration] etc. makes no sense; in fact, it limits and describes a traditionalist mind, and maybe even a tardo-positivist one, creating and imposing labels that effectively ghettoize, that are vaguely racist. (43)

He prefers instead "the term 'literature' full stop" ("l'appellativo di 'letteratura' e basta"), because, he goes on to say, "migrant literature represents and creates a perfect example of the 'world literature' of our time and gives our time purpose and meaning, no matter where." (43) Here, Gnisci is referring to that literary product of someone who is not Italian by birth but who lives in Italy and writes in Italian. At this point, overturning this geographic map and substituting his "migrant" writer in Italy with that writer who, in his turn, was born and raised in Italy but who later moved elsewhere and writes in Italian, we find ourselves with, analogically speaking, a type of doppelganger, a substitute, for that "migrant" writer whom Gnisci was discussing. In fact, Gnisci goes on to say, that "it isn't ever writers tout court who are thrown out into the jumble of the world from the void, *but writers in English, in Italian*, etc." (50; my italics) This insistence on the language is not arbitrarily restrictive; rather he sees it as the first step

---

[8] See the following two essays of mine: *Re-reading Italian Americana: Specificities and Generalities on Literature and Criticism* (Madison: Fairleigh Dickinson UP, 2014) ch. 1, 8; and "Appunti e notarelle sulla cultura diasporica degli Italiani d'America: ovvero, suggerimenti per un discorso di studi culturali," *Campi immaginabili* 34/35 (2007): 247-64.

[9] Two books come to mind in this regard: Iain Chambers, *Paesaggi migratori. Cultura e identità nell'epoca postcoloniale* (Meltemi, 2003, 2nd) and Cristina Lombardi-Diop and Caterina Romeo, eds., *L'Italia Postcoloniale* (Milan: Mondadori, 2014).

toward some kind of de-provincialization of the idea of the writer:

> To Italianize migrant writers literarily, therefore, means at the same time to Europeanize them, because Italy is part of a shared society made up of many nations that form a historic community as a result of conflicts and slaughter, but also consisting of a web of literature, art, culture, and taste that is unforgettable. (50)

And now our writer in the U.S. who writes in Italian, and who enjoys "a shared society" with those in Europe, in fact will be for us a writer "*in Italian*," as Gnisci said above: a writer in Italian who, when all is said and done, ends up being a writer "full stop" who writes "in Italian" even though not living in that geo-political region that is called Italy, but who knows it very well as a country and as a socio-cultural place within the contexts of Europe and of the United States where s/he goes about his/her own activities, personal and professional, in his/her everyday life.

What is said in this context is not so different, as we have said above, from what Piero Bassetti said regarding his concept of *italicità*. Bassetti described an Italic community as a "transnational community found, to varying extents, on all continents, and ... characterized by shared values and interests.[10] Not so different a community from the one proposed by Gnisci when he stated:

> I propose that, throughout the reading experience and the practice of writing and via a reciprocal transcultural co-evolution, foreign and migrant literary friends should try to promulgate along with us the idea of an Italian and European reform for them that would be critical and would not be refuted as being nationalist or assimilationist. (51)

So, for our writer the situation is, briefly, analogous to if not actually a reflection of the reform only from the geographic point of view. The person who writes in Italian in the United States experiences *de facto* a "transcultural evolution" that is, still naturally, "reciprocal" since she writes in Italian and, when possible, publishes in Italy with significant publishing houses. While it is not the sole factor, publishing in Italy does automatically put "into play," indeed, it demonstrates that there already existed "an Ital-

---

[10] See his "Italicity: Global and Local", 13. On the topic of the writer "in Italian" in the U.S., Bassetti states: "Historically, its roots lie in Italian emigration throughout the world, but it has since undergone many changes and now extends well beyond those roots."

ian reformation [and not only] European," but actually, American one, increasing the sources of an even larger reformation and, *in potentia*, richer for its creativity and criticality.[11]

Who, then, is this writer who will be discussed in this linguistic Italian context within a context greater than the geo-cultural territory that we know as the United States? He is undoubtedly a writer of Italian social and cultural upbringing, who writes in Italian but lives in the United States. He is even, in a rather obvious way, a writer who has much in common with other writers who work in Italian and live in Italy; which is, as Gnisci wrote, "a reciprocal transcultural co-evolution." Yet it is true that even if they have such a transcultural evolution in common, they remain different writers insofar as their relations depend on a series of characteristics that are simultaneously similar and different. And identity depends on this rapport between institutional/traditional and not,[12] similar in fact to what Charles Sanders Peirce says when he speaks of identity not as something founded on dissimilarity but, on the contrary, a state of being that distinguishes itself from another state that will certainly be similar to the first one but that possesses something unique; and so it has to do ultimately with a concept of identity that is perforce based on the hecceites of the individual.[13] And to underline the distinction between two things that are fairly similar but not the same, Peirce offers the following clarification:

> Two drops of water retain each its identity and opposition to the other no matter in what or in how many respects they are alike. Even could they interpenetrate one another like optical images (which are also individual),

[11] Some writers "(in) italian" who live in the United States are: Luigi Ballerini, *Se il tempo è matto* (poetry) Milan: Mondadori, 2010); Alessandro Carrera, *La vita meravigliosa dei laureati in lettere* (novel). Sellerio, 2002; Franco Ferrucci, *Lontano da casa* (novel) Turin: Einaudi, 1996); Luigi Fontanella, *Controfigura* (novel) (Venice: Marsilio, 2009); Pier Maria Pasinetti, *Piccole veneziane complicate* (novel) (Venice: Marsilio, 1996); Giose Rimanelli, *Tirò a piccione* (novel) (Turin: Einaudi, 1991, ristampa dell'edizione mondadoriana, 1951); Paolo Valesio, *Il cuore del girasole* (poetry) (Milan: Marietti, 2006).

[12] I direct the reader to Alain de Benoist, *Identità e comnuità* (Napoli: Guida, 2005).

[13] He says on this topic: "Otherness belongs to hecceities. It is the inseparable spouse of identity: wherever there is identity there is necessarily otherness; and in whatever field there is true otherness there is necessarily identity. Since identity belongs exclusively to that which is *hic et nunc*, so likewise must otherness." See his, *The Collected Papers of Charles Sanders Peirce*. Vols. I-VI ed. Charles Hartshorne and Paul Weiss (Cambridge, MA: Harvard UP, 1931-1935) 1.566.

> they would nevertheless react, though perhaps not at that moment, and by virtue of that reaction would retain their identities. (*Collected Papers* 1.458)

Two writers, therefore, who are not identical as writers but who nonetheless live either for the culture that has in some manner formed them, or for the language via which their work develops, as a result belong *sensu amplu* to a larger cultural-linguistic community that is, in general terms, Italian. Linked, in a Benoistian sense, even while different in a Peircean sense, the geographically Italian writers along with those who are linguistico-culturally Italian can be put back, so to speak, in that other category that Gnisci calls "writer (in) Italian." And so in this sense they are writers who are similar in many ways, but who also, owing especially to the fact that they inhabit two different geo-political areas, are distinct from one another like the drops of water that Peirce used as examples. They are therefore writers "in Italian" like the Italian writers (those who live and work in Italy) whom Gnisci adds to his "writers (in) Italian."

At this point we can turn again to Cometa's discourse, which—to appreciate once and for all the new critical and interpretive methodologies particularly with regard to these "new" writers—will need "to compel Italianists to a reformation of the canon and the canons that have been partially put forward in the last decades." This will extend as a result—and we might say necessity—what we maintain is Italian identity, which, as we have seen up to now, transforms itself into something that goes beyond the traditional and restrictive confines of such a concept, existing concomitantly with that concept (at this point customary but as of now no longer restricting and reductive) of "Italian writer" no matter where s/he lives.[14]

---

[14] As I have stated elsewhere, "…this results in a pluralistic notion of artistic invention and interpretation that, by its very nature, cannot exclude the individual—artist and reader/viewer—who has found 'a voice or style that does not violate [his or her] several components of identity'" (See my *Re-reading Italian Americana*, 38, where I reference Michael M. J. Fischer, "Ethnicity and the Post-modern Arts of Memory," in *Writing Culture: The Poetics and Politics of Ethnography*, ed. James Clifford and George E. Marcus [Berkeley: U of California P, 1986], 195).

I extend a special thanks to Sian Gibby of the John D. Calandra Italian American Institute for having provided an initial translation of this essay from Italian into English.

CONTRIBUTORS

MARY JO BONA is Professor of Italian American Studies and Women's and Gender Studies at Stony Brook University. She is past president of The Italian American Studies Association and serves on the board of MELUS, the Association of Multiethnic Literature of the United States. Her authored books include: *By the Breath of Their Mouths: Narratives of Resistance in Italian America*, *Claiming a Tradition: Italian American Women Writers*, and a book of poetry, *I Stop Waiting For You*. Bona is also editor of *The Voices We Carry: Recent Italian American Women's Fiction*; co-editor (with Irma Maini) of *Multiethnic Literature and Canon Debates*; and series editor of Multiethnic Literature for SUNY Press. Her manuscript, *Women Writing Cloth: Migratory Fictions in the American Imaginary*, examines representations of migratory women through the trope of needlework.

LEONARDO BUONOMO teaches American literature at the University of Trieste, Italy. He has served for two consecutive terms on the board of the Italian Association for North American Studies. His research interests include: nineteenth-century and early twentieth-century American writing, in particular the literary representation of Italy and Henry James's treatment of New York; Italian American writers; and American popular culture (especially American TV series). He is the author of *Backward Glances: Exploring Italy, Reinterpreting America (1831-1866)* (1996), *From Pioneer to Nomad: Essays on Italian North American Writing* (2003), and *Immigration, Ethnicity, and Class in American Writing, 1830-1860: Reading the Stranger* (2013). He is the president of the Italian American Association of Friuli Venezia Giulia.

MARINA CAMBONI is Professor of American Literature and Director of the PhD Program in Comparative Literature at the University of Macerata. Her fields of research are experimental poetry, Anglo-American modernism, cultural semiotics, translation and feminist theory. She has translated H.D.'s *Trilogy* (1993), selections of Adrienne Rich's poetry and prose (1985) and of Anne Sexton's poems (1990). She has extensively written on modernist writers (Virginia Woolf, Gertrude Stein, William Carlos Williams) and published books on Walt Whitman (*Il corpo dell'America: Leaves of Grass 1855*,1990; *Utopia in the Present Tense: Walt Whitman and the Language of the New World*, 1994; *Walt Whitman e la lingua del mondo nuovo*, 2004); H.D. (*H(ilda)D(oolittle) e il suo mondo*, 1995; *H. D.'s Poetry: "the meaning that words hide"* , 2003; *H.D. La donna che divenne il suo nome*, 2007). She has also edited the volume *Networking Women: Subjects, Places, Links Europe-America. For a Re-writing of Cultural History 1890-1939* (2004), and co-edited the volumes *USA: Identities, Cultures, and Politics in National, Trans-*

national and Global Perspectives (2009), and *Translating America. The Circulation of Narratives, Commodities, and Ideas Across the Atlantic* (2011). She served as AISNA President for the term 2007-2010 and as the Italian representative in the EAAS Board (2010-2013). A co-founder of the Transatlantic Walt Whitman Association (Paris 2007), and of the Italian-American Studies Network, she is at present working on a volume on Bryher and collaborating with the Walt Whitman Archive.

OTTORINO CAPPELLI teaches Political Science and Comparative Politics at the University of Naples "L'Orientale" and is Scholar in Residence at the John D. Calandra Italian American Institute, Queens College, CUNY where he directs the Maria Federici Oral History Archive. He has done extensive research on Italian-American politics and political elites and has published numerous essays on the subject both in English and Italian. His most recent book is *Italians in Politics in America. Conversations with Italian-American Legislators of the State of New York* (Calandra Institute, 2015). He is editor of and contributor to *Italian Signs, American Politics. Current Affairs, Historical Perspectives, Empirical Analyses* (Calandra Institute, 2012) and editor of with an introduction to *Cultura e politica nell'America italiana* (Cesati, 2015).

PETER CARRAVETTA is the Alfonse M. D'Amato Professor of Italian Studies at SUNY/Stony Brook. He has published on critical theory, postmodernism, migration, rhetoric, and cultural politics, and authors such as Vico, Nietzsche, Pasolini, Gertrude Stein, Lyotard, Eco. He has authored several books, including: *Prefaces to the Diaphora. Rhetorics, Allegory and the Interpretation of Postmodernity* (Purdue 1991), *The Elusive Hermes. Method, Discourse, Interpreting* (Davies Group 2013) and *La funzione Proteo. Ragioni della poesia e poetiche della fine* (Aracne 2014). His book *After Identity. Migration, Critique, Italian American Culture* is forthcoming from Bordighera Press.

MARGHERITA GANERI is Professor of Contemporary Italian Literature at the University of Calabria (Italy). She has published widely on Italian and Italian/American Literature and Criticism. She has been visiting professor at Cambridge University (UK), Stony Brook University (US), Italian School at Middlebury college (US), and other universities in Europe and Australia. In the current academic year 20014-15 she holds the University of Chicago's Fulbright Distinguished Chair in Italian Studies. Among her books: *Il romanzo storico in Italia. Il dibattito critico dalle origini al postmoderno* (Manni, 1999), *Pirandello romanziere* (Rubettino, 2001), *L'Europa in Sicilia. Saggi su Federico De Roberto* (Le Monnier, 2005), *L'America italiana. Epos e storytelling in Helen Barolini* (Zona, 2010), recently translated as *The Italian America. Epos and Storytelling in Helen Barolini* (Mimesis International, 2015).

FRED GARDAPHÉ is Distinguished Professor of English and Italian American Studies at Queens College, CUNY and the John D. Calandra Italian American Institute. He is past director of the Italian/American and American Studies Programs at Stony Brook University. His books include *Italian Signs, American Streets: The Evolution of Italian American Narrative*, *Dagoes Read: Tradition and the Italian/American Writer*, *Moustache Pete is Dead!*, *Leaving Little Italy*, and *From Wiseguys to Wise Men: Masculinities and the Italian American Gangster*, and *The Art of Reading Italian Americana*. With Giordano and Tamburri he is co-founder of Bordighera Press, publisher of *VIA: Voices in Italian Americana*. He is also editor of the Italian American Culture Series of SUNY Press.

PAUL GIORDANO is the Neil E. Euliano Professor and Chair of the Department of Modern Languages and Literatures at the University of Central Florida. At Loyola University Chicago he served as Chair of the Department of Modern Languages and as Director and Academic Dean of Loyola's Campus in Rome, Italy. He is past president of the American Association of Teachers of Italian. Among his publications are *From The Margin: Writings in Italian Americana* (Purdue UP, 2000 2nd ed.) with Tamburri and Gardaphé; *Beyond the Margin* (Fairleigh Dickinson UP, 1998) also with Tamburri; Joseph Tusiani: Poet Translator and Humanist An International Homage (Bordighera, 1994). Giordano has also published on the Renaissance and 20th century Italian literature. He is co-founder, with Tamburri and Gardaphé of Bordighera Press, publisher of the journal *Voices in Italian Americana*, and other book series. He also served as Associate Editor of *Italica*, the official publication of the American Association of Teachers of Italian.

DONATELLA IZZO is professor of American Literature at Università di Napoli "L'Orientale." She is past President of AISNA, the Italian Association of American Studies, and of the international Henry James Society, and is the general editor (with Giorgio Mariani and Stefano Rosso) of the international American Studies journal *Ácoma*. She has published widely on Henry James (*Portraying the Lady. Technologies of Gender in the Short Stories of Henry James* (UP of Nebraska, 2001) and on other 19th-century and 20th-century American writers, and edited or co-edited volumes and journal issues on literary theory, cross-cultural literary rewritings, American studies as a disciplinary field, Asian American literature and theory, American TV series, the graphic novel in the US, and the culture and politics of Hawai'i. In 2012, with Giorgio Mariani, she launched OASIS—Orientale American Studies International School—a biennial one-week school held on the isle of Procida, near Naples, and aimed at creating a new venue for conversations among Americanists from the U.S.A., southern Europe, North Africa, and the Middle East.

DJELAL KADIR is the Edwin Erle Sparks Professor of Comparative Literature, Emeritus, at Pennsylvania State University. He is the Founding President of the International American Studies Association and former Editor of the international quarterly *World Literature Today.* His authored books include: *Juan Carlos Onetti* (Twayne, 1977), *Columbus and the Ends of the Earth: Europe's Prophetic Rhetoric As Conquering Ideology* (U California P, 1992); *The Other Writing: Postcolonial Essays in Latin America's Writing Culture* (Purdue UP, 1993); *Questing Fictions: Latin America's Family Romance* (U Minnesota P, 1987) and *Memos from the Besieged City: Lifelines for Cultural Sustainability* (Stanford UP, 2011). He is the Co-editor of the *Routledge Companion to World Literature* (2012), the Co-Editor of *Literary Cultures of Latin America: A Comparative History*, 3 vols. (Oxford UP, 2004), of the *Longman Anthology of World Literature*, 6 vols. (2004). He is a Board member and teaching faculty member of the Institute for World Literature (Harvard).

CHRISTINA LOMBARDI-DIOP is the Director of the Rome Studies Program at Loyola University, Chicago, where she holds a joint appointment in the Modern Languages and Literatures Department, and the Women's Studies and Gender Studies Program. She has taught at the American University of Rome (2001-2008), Northwestern University (2008-2010) and the University of California, Berkeley (2011). Cristina is the recipient of numerous scholarly prizes (among which the Nonino Prize and the Prize of the American Association for Italian Studies). In 2014 she was nominated as finalist for the *Premio di Divulgazione Scientifica* awarded by the Italian Book Association. Her essays on white femininity and colonialism, Italian migrations, and African Italian diasporic literature, have appeared in a variety of edited volumes and journals. Among her most recent publications are the edited volume *Postcolonial Italy: Challenging National Homogeneity* (with Caterina Romeo, Palgrave, 2012) and the co-authored volume *Bianco e nero. Storia dell'identità razziale degli italiani*, with Gaia Giuliani (Le Monnier-Mondadori, 2013).

GIORGIO MARIANI is Professor of American Literature at the "Sapienza" University of Rome, where he coordinates the Doctoral Program in English-language literatures. Currently serving as President of the International American Studies Association (I.A.S.A.), he has also served as a member of the Executive Board of the Italian Association of North American Studies (A.I.S.N.A.). He is one of the co-editors of the Italian journal of American Studies *Ácoma*, as well as a member of the editorial boards of *Fictions* and *RIAS-The Review of international American Studies*. His work has concentrated on nineteenth-century American writers (Emerson, Melville, Stephen Crane, and others); on contemporary American Indian literature; on literary theory; on the literary and cinematic representation of war. He has published, edited, and co-edited several volumes, including:

Spectacular Narratives. Representations of Class and War in the American 1890s (1992), *Post-tribal Epics. The Native American Novel between Tradition and Modernity* (1996) and *Le parole e le armi* (words and arms), a collection of essays on U.S. discourses of war and violence from the Puritans to the first Gulf War. His essays and reviews have appeared in many journals, including *American Literary History, Studies in American Fiction, Fictions, RIAS, RSA Journal, Stephen Crane Studies.* His latest book is titled *Waging War on War: Peace fighting in American Literature*, and will be published by the University of Illinois Press later this year.

GRAZIELLA PARATI is the *Paul D. Paganucci Professor of Italian Language and Literature* and professor of comparative literature and women and gender studies at Dartmouth College, NH. She is the author of a number of books including *Migration Italy: The Art of Talking Back in A Destination Culture* (University of Toronto Press, 2005) and *Public History, Private Stories: Italian Women's Autobiographies*, (Minnesota UP, 1996). Her edited and coedited volumes include: *New Perspectives in Italian Cultural Studies: Definition, Theory, and Accented Practices* (Fairleigh Dickinson UP, 2012); *The Cultures of Italian Migration: Diverse Trajectories and Discrete Perspectives* (Fairleigh Dickinson UP, 2011); *Multicultural Literature in Contemporary Italy* (Fairleigh Dickinson UP, 2007); and *Mediterranean Crossroads: Migration Literature in Italy* (Fairleigh Dickinson UP, 1999).

JOSEPH SCIORRA is Director of Academic and Cultural Programs at the John D. Calandra Italian American Institute. He received his Ph.D. from the Department of Folklore and Folklife at the University of Pennsylvania. As a folklorist, Joseph has conducted ethnographic research with numerous New York City communities, in particular Italian Americans, implementing public programming such as museum exhibitions, concert series, and video documentaries, as well as publishing on religious practices, material culture, and vernacular music, among other topics. He is the editor of the social science and cultural studies journal *Italian American Review* and of *Italian Folk: Vernacular Culture in Italian-American Lives* (Fordham UP, 2011), co-editor of *Embroidered Stories: Interpreting Women's Domestic Needlework from the Italian Diaspora* (UP Mississippi, 2014) and *Graces Received: Painted and Metal Ex-votos from Italy* (Calandra Institute, 2012), and *Mediated Ethnicity* (Calandra Institute, 2010). Sciorra is the author of *R.I.P.: Memorial Wall Art* (Thames and Hudson, 1994, 2002), and *Built with Faith: Italian American Imagination and Catholic Material Culture in New York City* (U Tennessee P, 2015).

ANTHONY JULIAN TAMBURRI is Distinguished Professor of European Languages and Literatures and Dean of the John D. Calandra Italian American Institute. He is past president of the Italian American Studies Association and of the American Association of Teachers of Italian. His authored books include: *Una semiotica della ri-lettura: Guido Gozzano, Aldo Palazzeschi, Italo Calvino* (Cesati, 2003);

Narrare altrove: diverse segnalature letterarie (Cesati, 2007); *Una semiotica dell'etnicità: nuove segnalature per la letteratura italiano/americana* (Cesati, 2010); *Reviewing Italian Americana: Generalities and Specificities on Cinema* (Bordighera, 2011); and *Re-reading Italian Americana: Specificities and Generalities on Literature and Criticism* (Fairliegh Dickinson UP, 2014). His is co-editor for translations, with Robert Viscusi and James Periconi, of the English edition of *Italoamericana: The Literature of the Great Migration, 1880-1943* (Fordham UP, 2014); with Giordano and Gardaphé, *From The Margin: Writings in Italian Americana* (Purdue UP, 2000 2nd ed.); and other collections. He is executive producer and host of the TV program, *Italics*, and one of the co-founders of the Italian American Digital Project. He directs the Italian Series for Fairliegh Dickinson University Press.

MADDALENA TIRABASSI, Fulbright, is the Director of the Altreitalie Center on Italian Migration, Globus et Locus and editor of the journal *Altreitalie.* She is vice-president of AEMI (European Migration Institutions) in the advisory Board of the MEI (National Italian Museum on Emigration, Foreign Affaire Ministry), and consultant for the exhibition "Fare gli italiani" which celebrated Italian unification in 2011. Her main publications includes "Making Space for Domesticity. Household Goods in Working-Class Italian American Homes, 1900–1940," in Simone Cinotto (ed.), *Making Italian AmericaConsumer Culture and theProduction of Ethnic Identities* (New York: Fordham UP, 2014); with Alvise del Prà, *La meglio Italia. Le mobilità italiane nel XXI secolo* (Turin: Accademia UP, 2014); *I motori della memoria. Le donne piemontesi in Argentina*, 2010; *Itinera. Paradigmi delle migrazioni italiane*, ed. (Turin: Edizioni della Fondazione Giovanni Agnelli, 2005); *Il Faro di Beacon Street. Social Workers e immigrate negli Stati Uniti*, 1990. *Ripensare la patria grande. Amy Bernardy e le migrazioni italiane*, 2005; "Bourgeois Men, Peasant Women: Rethinking Domestic Work and Morality in Italy," in Donna, Gabaccia e Franca, Iacovetta, *Women, Gender and Transnational Lives* (Toronto: U Toronto P, 2002) 106-29.

ROBERT VISCUSI is professor of English and executive officer of the Wolfe Institute for the Humanities at Brooklyn College. The author of seven books and many scholarly articles, Viscusi has won an American Book award for his novel *Astoria*, the Premio Giuseppe Acerbi and the Fante/DiDonato Prize for his book *Buried Caesars and Other Secrets of Italian American Writing*, and the Brooklyn College Faculty Creative Writing Award for his internet epic *ellis island/ellisislandpoem.com.* Viscusi is chief editor of the American edition of Francesco Durante's anthology *Italoamericana: Literature of the Great Migration, 1880-1943* (Fordham UP, 2014).

Index

Index of Names